Interpreting
CHINA'S
ECONOMY

Gregory C Chow

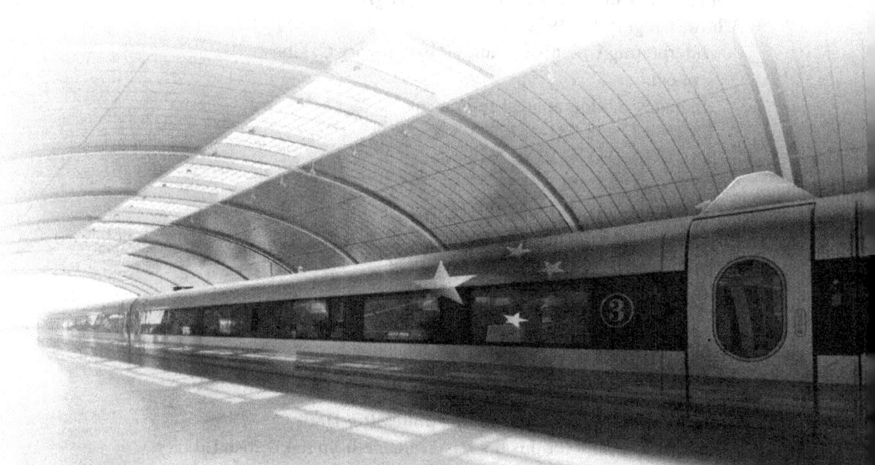

Interpreting CHINA'S ECONOMY

NEW JERSEY · LONDON · SINGAPORE · BEIJING · SHANGHAI · HONG KONG · TAIPEI · CHENNAI

Published by

World Scientific Publishing Co. Pte. Ltd.

5 Toh Tuck Link, Singapore 596224

USA office: 27 Warren Street, Suite 401-402, Hackensack, NJ 07601

UK office: 57 Shelton Street, Covent Garden, London WC2H 9HE

Library of Congress Cataloging-in-Progress Data

Chow, Gregory C., 1929–
Interpreting China's economy / by Gregory C. Chow.
p. cm.
Includes bibliographical references.
ISBN-13 978-981-4317-94-8 (hard)
ISBN-10 981-4317-94-2 (hard)
ISBN-13 978-981-4317-95-5 (pbk.)
ISBN-10 981-4317-95-0 (pbk.)
1. China -- Economic condictions -- 2000– 2. China -- Economic policy -- 2000–
I. Title.
HC427.95 .C49 2010

2010353549

British Library Cataloguing-in-Publication Data

A catalogue record for this book is available from the British Library.

First published 2010
Reprinted 2011

Typeset by Stallion Press
Email: enquiries@stallionpress.com

Printed in Singapore.

Preface

The essays of this book deal with important topics related to the Chinese economy. They are up-to-date and original. Most of them were published in Chinese in major newspapers in the last two years. A Chinese edition of this book 中国经济随笔 has been published by CITIC Press. Although written for the general reader, the essays are not casual comments but based on academic research and may benefit graduate and undergraduate students and professional economists. They result from more than 30 years of intensive study of and research on the Chinese economy and more than 40 years of experience in advising top government officials of Taiwan and the People's Republic of China on economic policy, economic reform and economics education.

In the process of studying China's economy I owe a great debt to students and colleagues at Princeton University and other major universities in the US and China that I have visited during this period, as well as friends in the government and the business community in mainland China, Hong Kong and Taiwan who have shared with me their understanding of China from

personal experience. I would like to acknowledge financial support from the Gregory C Chow Econometric Research Program of Princeton University for research on which many of the articles in this book are based. Critical comments from readers would be much appreciated.

Gregory C. Chow

Princeton, NJ

March, 2010

Contents

Part 1

Economic Development

1

Entrepreneurship Propelling Economic Changes in China

The most important aspect of the Chinese economy today is its rapid changes. These changes are propelled by the Chinese entrepreneurs. This essay is an attempt to understand who the entrepreneurs are, the environment in which they work, whether the dynamic changes will continue and what policies can be proposed to improve the changes.

For years the most important topic in the study of the Chinese economy was the economic reform led by the Chinese government and the Communist Party of China. See Chow (2007) on China's economic reform. Much of China's economic reform has been completed. The government has provided an environment in which entrepreneurs can thrive and change the economy for the better. To study the economic changes is to study the behavior of this group of economic actors. I assume that they are rational economic agents motivated by the pursuit of economic gains. Their behavior can be understood in the framework of maximization subject to the constraint of the environment. Although economic thinking applies to the present study, the propositions are qualitative rather than quantitative. Economic growth can be measured by such important variables as real GDP, but economic changes in China have qualitative aspects that I cannot and do not wish to describe completely in quantitative terms. Yet economic thinking will be used for the explanation and prediction of the changes and for suggesting policies to improve them.

Where do the most important changes take place? Who are responsible for these changes? What is the environment in which the entrepreneurs thrive? Will the changes continue? What are the policies for improving the changes in the future? These are the questions to be addressed in this paper.

1 Where do the Most Important Changes Take Place?

Starting with the basic classification of the production of goods and services in terms of consumption, investment and government expenditure, people responsible for economic changes are consumers, entrepreneurs, the government and the workers who produce the goods and services. All play their part in China's dynamic changes. I consider the most important changes to be the economic innovations for which the entrepreneurs are mainly responsible. If the reader disagrees that I have selected the most important changes, the objective of this essay remains to explain and predict the role of the Chinese entrepreneurs in making important changes in the Chinese economy.

Innovations have been occurring in many parts of the Chinese economy, from private enterprises producing consumer goods and services and producer goods to educational institutions providing educational services. Economists following the development of economics education in China are familiar with the innovations being introduced in certain top schools of economics in terms of organization, ways to motivate members of the faculty and staff, and methods of teaching and research. The successful enterprises making an important impact are numerous.

2 Who are Responsible for the Important Changes?

Given that the important changes are innovations, the people responsible are the entrepreneurs. The talents and areas of interest of these entrepreneurs vary, but all are self-made and all started with very little wealth. This is a main characteristic of the Chinese entrepreneurs. Simply because in the early 1980s all Chinese were poor, potential entrepreneurs started on a level playing field where no one had inherited wealth. This environment is a major factor in selecting the entrepreneurs who succeed mainly on account of their abilities.

To illustrate, several years ago while traveling in Wenzhou, I observed the operations of Mr Tiger's factory which produces cigarette lighters that dominate the world market. Mr Tiger was a worker who had been laid off by a state-owned enterprise and started making one or two cigarette lighters a day. He later created and managed an enterprise which at the time of my visit was occupying over a quarter of the world market. Another example is Dr Shi Zhengrong, who holds a PhD in physics. He returned to China from Australia in the late 1990s to start a company producing solar panels and was able, in five years, to make his company Suntech the second largest producer of solar panels in the world, second only to First Solar in the United States, while he himself became the richest person in China. As a third example, BYD Auto, based in Shenzhen, Guangdong Province, was established by its president Wang Chuanfu in 2003. It has sold 448,400 electric cars and, in December 2008, began selling the world's first mass-produced, plug-in hybrid vehicle, the BYD F3DM. In December 2008, Warren Buffet spent $230 million buying a 10% stake in the company.

These examples illustrate the variety of innovations occurring in China. In 2010, Forbes reported that China has 64 billionaires (excluding Hong Kong which has 25), including 27 new ones (implying an extremely rapid rate of increase), second only to the United States which has 403, or 40 percent of

the world total. Based on the list from http://www.forbes.com/lists/2010/10/billionaires-2010_The-Worlds-Billionaires_CountryOfCitizen_3.html, I have recorded the top six in Appendix A.

The businesses in which these six entrepreneurs are engaged include beverages, animal feed, retail, batteries and electric cars, and real estate, suggesting that one can succeed in a variety of businesses that provide consumer and producer goods. Three of the six had a college education while the remaining three did not. I was impressed by the two leading entrepreneurs in Taiwan and Hong Kong: Wang Yung-ching of Taiwan (who passed away two years ago) and Li Ka-shing of Hong Kong. Both did not have much education and started as low-paid workers but had excellent business skills and judgment. Many leading entrepreneurs in mainland China are of the same type.

3 What is the Environment in Which the Entrepreneurs Strive?

The environment will be discussed in terms of the following components.

3.1 The government

The government is contributing directly to economic changes but the present discussion is concerned with its role in providing an environment in which innovations by the entrepreneurs occur.

3.1.1

The Chinese government has provided a set of market institutions to enable the entrepreneurs to thrive. These institutions have well-known shortcomings but are good enough to allow the entrepreneurs to innovate. One institution is the enhanced legal status of entrepreneurs, from allowing entrepreneurs to join the Communist Party since the late 1990s to the March 14, 2004, constitutional amendment on private property stating that "legally obtained private property of the citizens shall not be violated."

3.1.2

Like other governments, the Chinese government has been building economic and social infrastructures to facilitate the entrepreneurs' work.

3.1.3

The Chinese government plays an important role in regulating the economic behavior of the entrepreneurs.

In establishing a new business and in operating an established business Chinese entrepreneurs need the approval of a set of bureaucrats, of the central government if the enterprise operates nationally or internationally and of the local government where the enterprise is located. Any bureaucrat along the way has an incentive to collect economic rent from the entrepreneur. Thus the entrepreneurs need to be skilled in dealing with government officials.

In the process of rent seeking, a Chinese government bureaucrat performs a useful function by selecting the able entrepreneurs whose undertakings require his approval. To maximize the present value of rents to be collected in the future, a bureaucrat will try to select the entrepreneurs who are most promising in running a profitable enterprise. Most bureaucrats themselves are intelligent. They are members of the Communist Party which has an indirect election process for selecting more talented people to serve at higher places although some are selected through personal favors and connections. Intelligent bureaucrats have an incentive to support the able entrepreneurs in order to increase future rents to be collected.

3.1.4

The Chinese government conducts macroeconomic policies to provide a stable economic environment for the entrepreneurs to strive in. In so doing, it is less subject to the influence of an independent legislature as in the US. This may affect the functioning of the Chinese macroeconomy and thus affect indirectly the environment of the entrepreneurs.

China has not experienced severe economic crises during the recent world economic downturn because its institutions are not allowed to take the large risks that American financial institutions could take. The issuers of derivative securities in the US are able to create financial assets whose values fluctuate greatly while the issuers are not required to have sufficient capital to bear the risk. The financial crisis in the US demonstrates that free exchange can lead to extreme risk taking and economic chaos. The Chinese government is slow in allowing financial derivatives to be introduced. Either by the act of the Chinese government or as a part of the nature of the Chinese people, Chinese consumers do not and cannot take as much risk as American consumers. They do not use credit excessively and spend money that they have not earned. The Chinese banking system is stable because it is mainly owned by the government; depositors do not worry about the safety of their deposits. Thus the economic environment in which the entrepreneurs strive is more stable than in the US in many respects.

3.2 China's market institutions

I treat the market institutions as a separate component of the environment because government policy is only one factor in the formation of China's market institutions. I single out free entry as an important aspect despite all the imperfections of China's market institutions. Free entry is demonstrated by the different kinds of entrepreneurs and the different types of innovations that have taken place. This aspect of economic freedom enables the Chinese entrepreneurs to thrive.

3.3 Chinese legal institutions

It is well recognized that a Western-style legal system is not being practiced in China although the Chinese legislature has introduced many laws similar to Western ones to facilitate the conduct of economic activities, especially by foreign investors. These laws are not strictly enforced. To be successful, Chinese entrepreneurs have to conduct business in the Chinese way, using *guanxi*, for example. They have the ability and are accustomed to doing this.

3.4 The Chinese culture in defining the rules of the game

Here, I use the term "culture" in a narrow sense. In a broad sense Chinese culture has affected both the behavior of the Chinese government and the Chinese legal institutions discussed above. In the narrow sense I refer to the cultural setting in which the Chinese entrepreneurs function. There are certain culturally acceptable ways of conducting business with partners and competitors and of treating employees. Social status is important for getting things done. Thus an able entrepreneur must invest in establishing a high social status. It is often observed that the US is ruled by law and China is ruled by people. One aspect of the rule by people is that those with high social status who are highly respected can get things done even without occupying a high position. Deng Xiaoping was the paramount leader of China for years without holding a very high position in the Chinese government.

The set of rules implicit from Chinese culture affect the way in which Chinese entrepreneurs establish their position in society, partly to make their economic activities more successful. In Hong Kong, for example, by contributing large sums to charity, entrepreneurs gain social status which is an important asset for getting things done.

3.5 Chinese workers

I do not refer to the abundance of Chinese workers that has led to low wages, an important factor in attracting foreign investment to China. (The relative wage in coastal provinces in China has increased so that some foreign investors have been moving to neighboring countries including India and Vietnam where wages are even lower.) I refer to the work ethic and skills that the

Chinese have inherited from thousands of years of market economic activities.

3.6 The Chinese entrepreneurs themselves

The Chinese entrepreneurs have their own characteristics, different from the characteristics of entrepreneurs elsewhere, because they are the result of thousands of years of Chinese history and culture as well as the recent history of turmoil and economic progress. I am not knowledgeable enough to give a complete account but can only mention a few relevant points.

Entrepreneurship has been developing for thousands of years since the market economy has existed for thousands of years. The quality and skill of Chinese entrepreneurs have been inherited from such a long historical tradition. Recent economic turmoil during the Great Leap Forward movement of 1958–61 and the Cultural Revolution of 1966–76, as well as the low standard of living during the period of economic planning up to 1978, has given the recent generation of Chinese the skill to survive and the strong desire to get rich. The recent economic growth shows the younger generation that opportunities are there for them to take. The intelligent entrepreneurs understand the environment and have the instinct and skill to take advantage of it. For example, many able Chinese entrepreneurs have taken advantage of the skill and diligence of workers by motivating them and giving them a sufficiently good set of working conditions.

4 Will the Changes Continue?

My answer is yes. Given the entrepreneurs' motivation to succeed and the favorable environmental conditions, we can predict a continuation of their behavior and of similar successful changes in the future. This prediction will be proven wrong only if the motivation or ability of the entrepreneurs change (which is extremely unlikely) or if the environment becomes less favorable.

Topping the list of possible changes in the environment for the worse is the possibility that the opportunity for innovation will vanish. Schumpeter (1947, p. 124) predicted that the "perfectly bureaucratized giant industrial unit ... ousts the entrepreneur and expropriates the bourgeoisie as a class which in the process stands to lose ... its function." This has not happened to the Chinese entrepreneurs who keep on innovating and creating new firms as described in this paper. In the foreseeable future, opportunities for innovation in China and in the rest of the world will still be there for one reason alone. Future increase in output will require the use of energy and environmental resources that will damage the environment unless new methods of production are found to increase the output/energy ratio or to provide new methods of utilizing alternative sources of energy to fossil fuel. The opportunity and the need for innovation for this purpose is unlimited. Economic progress damages the natural environment unless new ways of producing and consuming are found that are friendly to the environment.

Now let me turn to other obstacles. These obstacles can be logically classified as obstacles occurring in the different components of the environment in which the entrepreneurs operate, as listed in Section 3.

The most often discussed is the instability of the Chinese government. Different observers have different opinions concerning its possible instability. Pessimists may point to serious problems facing the Chinese government, including problems of rural poverty and income inequality, the shortcomings of a one-party political system, the deterioration of healthcare provision for a large number of people in the rural area, the corruption of government officials, etc. Space constraints do not allow me to discuss each of these possibly destabilizing factors. A reader having a strong opinion on the possible instability of the Chinese government will answer the question in this section differently. On the issue of rural poverty and income inequality, the reader may refer to Chow (2009a).

One can go through the list of components of the environment facing the Chinese entrepreneurs. If a reader can find an important reason for that component to become unfavorable to entrepreneurship, his projection will be different from what I have stated.

Such differences are similar to projections based on econometric models. Different economists may select different sets of variables to be included in a model and specify different ways in which the selected variables interact to give forecast. I have described the economic actors and their environment and use this description (or model, if it were quantitative) to predict the behavior of the actors in the future. Unless there are some basic changes in the way the actors function or in their environment, my prediction should be valid.

5 What Policies Could Improve the Changes in the Future?

I could go through each component of the environment listed above to suggest how they can be improved. Since the list covers many aspects of the Chinese economy, only selected policy recommendations will be included.

5.1 Government

Many observers agree that the Chinese government has done a good job in carrying out economic reform to provide a set of market institutions and in providing social and economic infrastructures for the entrepreneurs to thrive. One can always point to specific reform measures or infrastructure building that can be improved. Certain large government projects such as the Western Development involve waste and corruption and can be improved.

I have pointed out the positive side of having government bureaucrats selectable entrepreneurs to support in the process of collecting economic rents. The negative side is the inefficiency of having so many layers of bureaucrats who have the authority to interfere with the working of the entrepreneurs. This is well-known by the leadership of the Chinese government but it is not easy to improve this. An able leader like Zhu Rongji was once able to streamline the Chinese government to some extent, but if such an able leader is not present today to streamline the procedures for the entrepreneurs, a recommendation by an economist is fruitless. The same remark applies to the widespread corruption in China. Corruption is recognized by the Chinese government. The Communist Party leadership has asserted repeatedly that it is their top priority to reduce or control corruption. They do not need to be reminded that this is an important task.

In the conduct of macroeconomic policies, the Chinese government seems to have done a reasonably good job. The Chinese economy is thriving while most of the world is experiencing economic stagnation. It is easy to suggest some improvements, such as allowing the value of the RMB to be subject to the determination of market forces to a larger extent. I believe that the rigidity of the exchange rate is mainly the result of political considerations in China. It is risky for a top Chinese government official to allow the exchange rate of the RMB to appreciate rapidly because a significant, vocal segment of the population would object. A more feasible policy change is to use a large quantity of China's foreign exchange reserve for China's economic development, such as the development of the western region. The increase in the supply of US dollars resulting from such an undertaking will naturally lower the exchange value of the dollar relative to the RMB. Allowing the appreciation of the RMB in such a process may be politically more acceptable.

5.2 Market institutions

The Chinese government has established market institutions through economic reform. The next step is to allow more freedom for market institutions to evolve by themselves, mainly through the effort of entrepreneurs. Given sufficient economic freedom, suitable market institutions have evolved naturally around the world. Some examples are the stock markets in New York and in Shanghai during the 1920s which were not set up by the government.

5.3 Legal institutions

China's legal system has improved a great deal, such that citizens are now allowed to sue the government, but in practice the legal system often favors the government in settling disputes. Furthermore, some lawyers are punished because they actively pursue legal action against the government. This is one aspect of the Chinese political system with a high concentration of government power in certain areas which the government is not willing to give up. Observers, including respected scholars in China, believe that giving up power and relaxing control of the population in a number areas and treating all parties in a legal dispute as equal under the law would be good for China and for the Communist Party itself, but top leaders may not agree and are not willing to take these bold steps.

5.4 Culture

The culture can only change slowly. The Chinese government considers it to be its responsibility to educate or rally the population to work for the good of the country. This being the case, the government can influence the people by increasing and improving civic education in schools and by promoting the Chinese culture as it has been doing to a limited extent.

5.5 Workers

I treat this component as part of investment in human capital. There are ways in which the government can improve the formation of human capital by improving the education system and healthcare system and by allowing smooth migration of the labor force. The system of higher education is subject to tighter control than necessary or desirable. For example, the regulation of movement of faculty members should be more decentralized. There should be no need to get approval from the Ministry of Education when a university professor wishes to travel abroad. For the healthcare system, the supply of healthcare in China has remained stagnant for years since the mid-1990s while almost all consumer goods and services have increased at rapid rates. This is mainly because of the monopoly on healthcare supply by local governments which are interested in spending their revenue on urban development. Allowing and protecting the free entry of private healthcare can help increase the supply and improve the quality of healthcare, thus improving the quality of human capital in China. This topic is discussed in Chow (2009b).

5.6 The entrepreneurs themselves

The entrepreneurs have been doing an excellent job in promoting economic changes for the betterment of China. Perhaps they can be persuaded to take a more active role in promoting the collective welfare of the country, such as contributing to activities for the common good, beyond what self-interest can achieve through the invisible hand of the market. Like anyone else, entrepreneurs can improve their spirit of service by self-education and through social action. The Chinese people have demonstrated their willingness to help others during disasters like the earthquake in Sichuan Province in 2008.

6 Summary

This essay has described the Chinese entrepreneurs as a group and the environment in which they thrive, explained why successful innovation will continue and suggested some policies that may help entrepreneurship thrive even better in the future.

References

Chow, Gregory C. *China's Economic Transformation*, 2nd edition. Oxford: Blackwell Publishing, Ltd., 2007.

Chow, Gregory C. "Rural poverty in China: problem and solution," in Ravi Kanbur and Xiaobo Zhang, eds., *Governing Rapid Growth in China: Equity and Instituions.* New York: Routledge, 2009a, pp. 229–246.

Chow, Gregory C. "An Economic Analysis of Health Care in China," in Gordon G. Liu, Shufang Zhang and Zongyi Zhang, eds., *Investing in Human Capital for Economic Development in China.* Singapore: World Scientifi c, 2009b.

Schumpeter, Joseph A. *Capitalism, Socialism and Democracy.* New York: Harper and Brothers Publishers, 1947.

Appendix A: Top Six Richest Persons in China from Forbes' List

#103 Zong Qinghou

Net Worth:	**$7.0 bil**
Fortune:	Self-made
Source:	Beverages
Age:	64
Country of Citizenship:	China
Residence:	Hangzhou
Education:	NA
Marital Status:	Married, 1 child

Mainland China's richest person. He started a beverage business in a mini-grocery in a school in Hangzhou in 1986, targeting picky children and their parents. The company name sounds like an infant's laugh. He formed a joint venture with Danone in 1996; partnership unraveled amid a dispute over the right to use the Wahaha brand, leading to bitter lawsuits. Detente took place in September 2009 when Wahaha agreed to buy out Danone's interests for an undisclosed amount. This hasn't hurt sales: now China's biggest beverage maker selling bottled water, tea drinks, juice and coffee, Wahaha's 2009 revenues are estimated at $6.3 billion.

#154 Liu Yongxing

Net Worth:	**$5.0 bil**
Fortune:	Self-made
Source:	Feed
Age:	62
Country of Citizenship:	China
Residence:	Shanghai
Education:	NA
Marital Status:	Married, 1 child

With $120 in savings, he and three brothers got started raising quails and chickens in 1982. Their Hope Group became one of China's largest makers of animal feed. The siblings split in 1995; Yongxing moved to Shanghai. His privately held East Hope Group is still one of China's biggest feed producers, making 100 types; the core feed business has done well amid rising demand for meat in China as household incomes rise. The company is looking to expand in southern Vietnam. He also owns aluminum smelters and is investing in the plastics industry in China. His only son Shawn, a graduate of the University of Southern California, is heir apparent; his wife is from Texas.

#176 Zhang Jindong

Net Worth:	**$4.5 bil**
Fortune:	Self-made
Source:	Retail
Age:	47
Country of Citizenship:	China
Residence:	Nanjing
Education:	Nanjing Normal University, Bachelor of Arts/Science
Marital Status:	Married

A Chinese literature major, he worked as a manager in a state-owned company before striking out on his own in the air-conditioning wholesale market in his native Nanjing in 1990. He soon shifted to retail. Using his $12,000 in savings, he opened his first store with 200 square meters of floor space. Now, China's second largest electronics retailer is benefiting from the double-digit growth in the nation's retail spending; shares are up by 50% in the past year. One of Forbes Asia's 2009 "Fab 50" best large businesses in Asia, Suning bought Hong Kong appliance retailer Citicall Retail Management in February. His elder brother, property developer Zhang Guiping, is also a billionaire.

#189 Wang Chuanfu

Net Worth:	**$4.4 bil**
Fortune:	Self-made
Source:	Batteries, electric cars
Age:	44
Country of Citizenship:	China
Residence:	Shenzhen
Education:	Beijing Non-Ferrous Research Institute, Master of Science; Central South Industrial University of Technology, Bachelor of Arts/Science
Marital Status:	Married

His BYD Co. is now one of China's top automakers. He began selling electric cars in December 2008, just a few months after Warren Buffett's MidAmerican Energy bought a 10% stake in the firm, a move that helped push up stock sixfold in 10 months. He hopes to start selling models in the US in 2010. The company also makes batteries and battery chargers; its stock tumbled this fall after its 65%-owned subsidiary BYD Electronics recalled the battery chargers it supplied to Nokia due to potential electric shocks. He left his post at a government-affiliated research institute in Beijing in 1995 to co-found BYD

Co. with Lu Xiangyang, now also a billionaire. Wu was initially a rechargeable battery manufacturer. In 2003 BYD acquired a state-owned, mid-size automaker in Xian.

#212 Hui Ka Yan

Net Worth:	**$4.0 bil**
Fortune:	Self-made
Source:	Real Estate
Age:	51
Country of Citizenship:	China
Residence:	Guangzhou
Education:	Wuhan U of Science & Tech, Bachelor of Arts/Science; Wuhan University, Bachelor of Arts/Science
Marital Status:	Married

A property developer, he took his Evergrande Real Estate public in Hong Kong in November, raising $730 million; for a brief time, he was China's richest person. Shares have since fallen from their peak. Early investors in the offering included Hong Kong billionaire Joseph Lau's Chinese Estates Holding, Hong Kong billionaire Cheng Yu-tung's Chow Tai Fook and Singapore's Temasek Holdings. The company raised another $750 million in January, selling its five-year debt at a 13% interest rate. He earned his bachelor's degree in metallurgy in 1982 from Wuhan University of Science and Technology; and has served as adjunct professor there since 2003. He shares wealth with his wife.

#232 Wu Yajun and family

Net worth:	**$4.0 bil**
Fortune:	Self-made
Source:	Real Estate
Age:	46

Country of Citizenship:	China
Residence:	Chongqing
Education:	NA
Marital Status:	Married

The chief executive of real estate developer Longfor Properties, which she co-founded with her husband Cai Kui, who shares the fortune. The company went public on the Hong Kong stock exchange in November 2009; cornerstone investors included Ping An Insurance, Temasek Holdings and the Singapore government. She has a degree in navigation engineering. She worked at Qianwei Meter Factory from 1984 to 1988; spent the next five years working as a journalist and editor at the China Shirong News Agency. Shortly after that, she began developing real estate in her hometown of Chongqing. Now her firm has property in Beijing and other large cities.

2

China's Economic Reform: Retrospect and Prospect

I feel very fortunate to be able to attend the 5th Annual Meeting of Economists in China. I am excited about returning to China at this time. Recalling my return to China for the first time in 1980 when I gave lectures in econometrics in the Summer Palace in Beijing, I cannot help noticing the tremendous progress that has taken place in China. I express my admiration to all of you for your important contributions to the promotion of economics education and research in China. In particular, Professor Hai Wen should be recognized for his leadership in organizing these annual meetings for Chinese economists. This is the first time I am attending these annual meetings but I recognize their importance in promoting economics education and research in China.

The topic I have chosen for today's discussion is China's economic reform. I hope to exchange views with you on three aspects: the reform of state-owned enterprises, the reform of non-state enterprises and the open-door policy.

First, public assets were once controlled under central planning, including the communes and state-owned enterprises. What enabled these public assets to function effectively in the environment of a market economy? A simple answer is "the responsibility system." In the communes, when the farm households were given responsibility to farm the land assigned to them, they could get additional wealth through hard work. In industrial production, state enterprises were turned over to the management, separating the ownership, which is public, and the management, which is private. Efficiency increased because the management and workers could benefit from their ingenuity and hard work. Management was in fact maximizing profits as in a well-functioning market economy.

Second, concerning the non-state-owned assets, I believe the most important policy was to allow them the freedom to develop as they pleased. This accounted for the dynamic growth of the township and village enterprises, to the extent that leader Deng Xiaoping had not anticipated. The central government was wise to allow these enterprises to flourish freely. The same applies to the policy to allow private educational institutions to develop alongside the public schools.

Third, the open-door policy was a 180-degree turn from the previous policy to restrict foreign investment and foreign trade. Local government and, later, private and foreign enterprises were allowed to engage in foreign trade and foreign investment. Foreign investment has contributed significantly to economic growth, in providing the needed financial and physical capital and the new technology associated with the inflow of capital, in introducing modern management skills, in the training of Chinese workers, and in setting up a new system of business practices. However, foreign investment is not a fundamental factor in the sense that China had the basic economic conditions and environment favorable for attracting foreign investment which could have gone anywhere in the world.

Next, I would like to suggest how these three aspects of economic reform could be further improved.

In the case of state-owned enterprises, the responsibility system is not sufficient. These enterprises were transformed into share-holding companies in the late 1990s. Shares of the small and medium-sized enterprises were held by employees and these enterprises function efficiently. The shares of large enterprises were held publicly. The management was still appointed by the bureaucrats who controlled the shares and many still had monopoly power in the industry. The management of public assets by bureaucrats has led to corruption, and, even worse, to the misallocation of valuable economic resources. An outstanding example is the public ownership of land. The bureaucrats who have the power to approve the use of public land not only collect illegal fees in the approval of its use but also have no incentive to limit its use in order for use in the future when returns would be higher. Besides the misallocation of this valuable resource, the system of public land ownership has led to the overheating of the macroeconomy in the form of excessive urban development.

Second, on the development of non-state enterprises, the legal status of these enterprises and the ability of entrepreneurs to function can still be improved. These enterprises were able to flourish mainly because the Chinese entrepreneurs were able and willing to take risk in politically unfavorable environments. (Since the writing of this paper in 2005, the environment facing private entrepreneurs has improved.)

This is the time to allow economic institutions to develop freely in the environment of a market economy. Economic reform took place under government direction. New institutions were developed by the government, including the stock markets in Shanghai and Shenzhen. In a market economy, suitable institutions, like the stock markets in New York and in Shanghai in the 1920s and 1930s, were developed naturally by entrepreneurs who saw the economic need for such institutions. In terms of economic reform, the work of the central government should also allow the market to compete in the formation of new institutions just as it allowed private enterprises to compete with state-owned enterprises in the pursuit of profits.

Finally, the open-door policy. It is China's participation in the globalization of the world economy. Globalization allows the free flow of goods, financial and physical capital and the associated technology and people. China's accession to the WTO in 2001 was a great step taken for China to become a member of the world economic community. Premier Zhu Rongji promoted China's WTO membership mainly to encourage foreign competition in order to improve the efficiency of many bureaucratically run state-owned enterprises. I believe that at the present stage, Chinese banks should be allowed to face more foreign competition, and the exchange rate of the RMB should be allowed to be market determined to a larger extent. At the same time I recognize that allowing economic globalization to take place slowly in China has its advantages and the Chinese government should be complimented in this regard. The proper speed of economic changes is a delicate matter. By and large the Chinese government has handled this matter quite successfully.

Since the Chinese government has successfully transformed the economy to a market economy to a large extent, we can expect that further reform will be slow and limited. On the other hand, rapid economic growth will continue in China because the three fundamental driving forces are and will still be operating in the foreseeable future. As pointed out in my book *China's Economic Transformation*, the abundance of high-quality human capital, including the ingenious and resourceful entrepreneurs and the hardworking and skillful labor force, a set of well-functioning though imperfect market institutions and the large technology gap between a large part of China and the most advanced economies give China and other less developed economies room to catch up. We can expect a prosperous and rapidly growing Chinese economy for some time to come.

3

Review of China's Economic Development in the 20 years Since 1989

Twenty years have elapsed since the tragic Tiananmen incident of June 4, 1989. It is an opportune moment for *Hong Kong Economic Monthly* to take stock of the development of the Chinese economy in these two decades.

On June 14, 1989, I was invited to speak to a gathering of Princeton University alumni in Hong Kong on the prospects of economic growth in China, an event scheduled before the Tiananmen incident. While experiencing extreme sadness for the incident, I expressed the view that it would slow down the rapid economic growth of China only slightly because economic growth depends on fundamental economic factors as long as law and order is maintained. The economic fundamentals are the high-quality human capital, a set of functioning market institutions and China's being in early stage of economic development. Human capital includes the skillful and hardworking labor force and the resourceful and ingenious entrepreneurs. The market institutions may be imperfect but are good enough to enable the workers and entrepreneurs to strive to improve their economic wellbeing. Being in an early stage of development, China can adopt the most advanced technology available and leapfrog in its economic development. These were the same factors that had enabled the rapid economic growth of Japan before and after World War II, and of Hong Kong, Singapore, Taiwan and South Korea in the 1960s and 1970s. These three fundamental economic factors had already propelled mainland China's economic growth up to 1989 and has continued to do so ever since.

1 Accomplishments

Let me first review the economic accomplishments since 1989. With 1978 = 100, the index of real GDP in China grew from 271.3 in 1989 to 1500.7 in 2007 (*China Statistical Yearbook 2008*, Table 2–5), or at an average annual rate of about 10 percent per year. In the 11 years between 1978 and 1989, the rate of growth of real GDP had been about 9.5 percent. Some may question the accuracy of Chinese official national income statistics but we need only to look at some glaring facts to be assured of China's economic growth. The over 4000 skyscrapers in Shanghai built since the early 1990s are there for everyone to see. For the country as a whole, housing space increased from 13.5 square meters in 1989 to 27.1 square meters in 2007 per urban resident, and from 17.2 square meters in 1989 to 31.6 square meters in 2007 per rural resident. In 2007 there were 165 mobile phones per 100 urban residents and 78 mobile phones per hundred rural residents. In 2008 China produced over 11 million automobiles, just surpassing the output in the United States. High-quality Chinese products are sold in the world market, from toys and shoes in 1989 to computers and automobiles in more recent years. China has accumulated US$2 trillion in foreign reserves from its trade surpluses.

2 Role of the Open-Door Policy

The open-door policy of Deng Xiaoping enabled such a rapid growth to take place. Foreign investment, to which the residents of Hong Kong contributed significantly, played an important role in the growth process. It provided China with financial and physical capital, modern management skills and practices, and competition for domestic enterprises to increase their efficiency. China's state enterprises were known to be inefficient. However, when subject to foreign competition, some of them became efficient if the management was given sufficient reward to do a good job. An obvious example is the performance of Dongfang 东方 Hotel in Guangzhou. It improved greatly in the mid-1980s when facing competition from the Hong Kong-invested and managed hotels including the White Swan, China Hotel and Garden Hotel. However, foreign investment is not a fundamental factor in China's rapid economic growth. International investors could have put their money anywhere in the world. They chose to invest in China because of the favorable economic environment created by the three economic fundamentals that I have listed above.

A similar remark can be made about the role of foreign trade. The opportunities to export enabled China to produce in exchange for goods needed in China, but China had to be able to produce these commodities in the first place. In 1989 China was still running a trade deficit and its exports accounted for only 11 percent of GDP. China began running a trade surplus in 1990 and by 2006 its exports accounted for 35 percent of its GDP. Why were China's exports so limited until the 1990s? It was the same economic fundamentals that enabled China to improve its technology up to a point when its exports were desired in the world market. Foreign observers have attributed China's export surplus in recent years to an undervalued RMB. The exchange rate of a country's currency is a factor affecting its trade surplus and deficit, but without the ability to produce exports of good quality and at low cost, a country cannot benefit from foreign trade simply by undervaluing its currency.

3 Role of the Non-State Sectors

Besides the open-door policy, an important component of economic policy was to allow and encourage the development of non-state sectors while the state sector was being transformed gradually. China did not take the route later taken by the Soviet Union to privatize the inefficient state-owned enterprises in 500 days. Rather, the government transformed these enterprises gradually while allowing and encouraging non-state enterprises to flourish. The township and village enterprises became the most dynamic driving force of the economy up to the mid-1990s. Foreign and domestic enterprises also experienced rapid growth. In the early 1980s almost all Chinese citizens were poor. Starting from an almost equal footing economically, the resourceful entrepreneurs were able to succeed. In addition to establishing new businesses of their own, many former managers of state and collective enterprises were given ownership of these enterprises through the years. In the late 1990s, state-owned enterprises became shareholding companies. Shares of the small and medium-sized state enterprises were sold to the staff and workers. This increased the capital of the enterprises and provided incentives for the workers and staff. Most of the shares of the large state enterprises remained publicly held but more and more were traded in the Shenzhen and Shanghai stock markets and later in the Hong Kong and New York stock markets. Thus, privatization of state-owned enterprises was gradual and by and large effective, while the economy was being moved forward by collective, foreign and private enterprises.

4 Income Inequality

Has the increase in wealth spread to the poor people in China? The answer is yes. Although the urban population has benefited much more, the improvement in income of the rural population has been substantial. The index of per capita annual real disposable income (with 1978 = 100) increased from 198.1 in 1990 to 752.3 in 2007 for the urban population, and from 311.2 to 734.4 for the rural population (*China Statistical Yearbook 2008*, Table 9–2). The average annual rate of increase was 8.2 percent for the former and 5.2 percent for the latter. Note from the above indices that between 1978 and 1990, the increase in per capita income for the rural population was much higher than for the urban population. While the improvement of living standards for the rural population has been substantial, income inequality has increased simply because the rates of increase in income of the two groups were different. In 2007 per capita income of the urban population was 13,786 yuan as compared with 4,140 yuan for the rural population or 3.3 times as much.

Poverty as measured by the percentage of population below a certain poverty line has been reduced rapidly. If we define the poverty line as having an income of 600 yuan or less in 2006 prices, the percentage of the Chinese population below this poverty line has decreased substantially from 12 percent in 1985 to 9 percent in 1990, 3.5 percent in 2003 and 1.8 percent in 2006 (*China Statistical Yearbook 2008,* Table 9-19 and similar tables of earlier *Yearbooks*).

5 Problems in the Rural Economy

Other than poverty there are other problems in the Chinese rural economy. The government has emphasized three aspects of the rural problem (farms, farmers and farming). Concerning the problem of farms, the government has spent less on infrastructure investment in rural areas than in urban areas. Concerning the problem of farmers, it has provided less welfare benefits, including healthcare and education subsidies, to rural residents than to urban residents. Although much labor mobility is allowed for farmers to move to urban areas to find work, those working in the urban areas are subject to discrimination under the government policy (introduced in the 1950s) of separating the residence status of the urban and rural populations. The entitled benefits are associated with the residence status. The migrating workers do not have residence permits in the cities and cannot use services such as healthcare and schooling for their children. Concerning the problem of farming, the government has invested only a limited amount to improve agricultural productivity. In addition, in the procurement of farm products, government agencies have set the procurement prices below market prices while the farmers are not allowed to sell grain to private traders.

The most serious problem for the farmers is not the poverty or lack of welfare benefits but the violation of their rights by illegal activities of local government and Party officials. The most disconcerting example is the confiscation of land contracted to farmers for urban development, for which many farmers receive a compensation that is arbitrary and well below market price. Second, many rural residents are not paid, or not paid on time, for work performed such as on public works and teaching in public schools. Third, farmers are subject to illegal levies. The levies include the increase in tax on the reported acreage of the farmer's land above the acreage actually used, a special tax for growing commercial crops besides grain and livestock feed, and fees for schools, road construction and other services provided by the local government. One reason for the extra levies is the tax reform of 1994 which increased the proportion of government revenue paid to the central government (from 22.0 percent in 1993 to 55.7 percent in 2004) at the expense of provincial and local governments which needed to raise the additional revenue. Another reason is the central government's policy to assign to local governments the responsibility of providing nine years of "compulsory education" and adequate healthcare. In 2006, the government decided to abolish all taxes on farmers in order to make it more difficult for local officials to impose levies of their own. The mistreatment of farmers by local Party officials remains a serious problem.

6 Corruption

The mistreatment of farmers by Party officials is one aspect of corruption. Corruption is a serious problem in China. It occurs when government or Party officials exercise the power of their position for their own benefit. They are paid for their services required to approve and facilitate economic activities.

These include the establishment and operation of enterprises, the issuance of import and export licenses, the approval of the production and sale of medicine, and the use of public land for construction. When such economic activities increased during rapid economic growth, the demand for the services of government officials also increased. Therefore corruption has increased. A second component of corruption is the embezzlement of government assets by officials in government-owned economic institutions. There are known cases of officials of state-owned banks transferring very large sums of money to their private accounts. Because of widespread corruption, many Chinese people have lost confidence in the government while some have accepted it passively as a reality.

Realizing the harmful effects of corruption, the leadership of the Chinese Communist Party has made serious attempts to control it by punishing serious offenders severely. Such attempts have not been successful. An effective way to reduce corruption would be to limit the source of economic power of government officials. One form of economic power is the regulation of economic activities by the government, but government regulation in many cases, such as the approval of a new medicine, serves a useful purpose even though it is also a key source of corruption in China. Another source of economic power is derived from the public ownership of land that requires the approval of government officials for its use, but public ownership of land is a basic doctrine of the Communist Party that is difficult to change. Under these circumstances, corruption in China is likely to remain in the foreseeable future.

Readers are fully aware that Hong Kong has succeeded in eliminating corruption. Is there any lesson that the Chinese government can learn from Hong Kong's successful experience? Hong Kong government officials are much better paid. Since Hong Kong is small, any misbehavior by a government official, when exposed, will be subject to social sanction by the entire population.

The Hong Kong media is free to expose the misbehavior of high-level government officials. The rule of law has been practiced in Hong Kong for a long time and an effective anti-corruption institution can be build upon this social tradition.

7 Healthcare

A second economic problem is the provision of healthcare. In the midst of rapid progress in all other aspects of economic life, healthcare provision stands as a glaring exception. In terms of quality, many rural residents do not enjoy the same level of healthcare that they used to enjoy when it was provided freely in the communes. After the collapse of the commune system, healthcare was no longer freely provided as barefoot doctors started their own private practice. In terms of quantity, a striking fact is that the amount of healthcare provided to the Chinese population did not increase between 1995 and 2003 while the consumption of all other goods and services increased rapidly. A comprehensive measure of healthcare provision is the total expenditure on healthcare in constant prices. It is obtained by dividing the expenditure in nominal terms by the price index of medical services (=1.00 for 1995 and =2.616 for 2003). Total medical expenditure in China was 225. 78 billion yuan in 1995 and was only 251.69 billion yuan in 2003 after being divided by the above price index. There was practically no increase in per capita terms if we allow for the increase in population during this period. Other measures such as the number of hospital beds, medical personnel and medical doctors per 10,000 persons also showed no increase.

Why has there been no increase in healthcare provision? Under China's constitution the provision of healthcare is the responsibility of the government, and the central government delegated this responsibility to local governments. The local governments have preferred to spend their revenue on other purposes such as developing the local economy while maintaining the level of healthcare supply at a level which they deem sufficient. A simple and effective way to increase healthcare supply and to improve its quality is for the central government to encourage private provision, but this has not been done because of the vested interests of current local health officials.

Turning from the supply side of healthcare to the demand side, an important issue is how to establish an insurance system to pay for it. The Chinese government has tried to increase healthcare insurance coverage for both the urban and the rural populations. For the rural population, the government has made a serious effort to get them to join a form of medical insurance known as the collective medical system (CMS). The total annual cost per person is 50 yuan, out of which the central and local government each pays 20 yuan, leaving 10 yuan to the family. In April 2009 the Central Committee of the CCP and the State Council jointly announced a very ambitious healthcare plan costing 850 billion RMB, partly to raise the insurance subsidy by government at all levels to 120 yuan per person in 2010 for both the urban and rural populations. How successful this program will be remains to be seen. In the past many rural residents refused to join the government insurance system even when the system was highly subsidized because they did not believe they would actually receive medical care as stipulated when they needed it. The 2009 plan also includes the construction of 29,000 township hospitals and the upgrading of 5000 township hospitals in 2009, as well as the construction of village clinics.

There was a discussion in Beijing on the most effective way to improve healthcare, whether to increase insurance coverage or to subsidize the building of hospitals and clinics. By increasing insurance coverage, if a hospital serves the public well, it will automatically receive such subsidies from the patients who choose to go there. The 2009 announcement showed that the government has decided on this issue by subsidizing both. Given the serious attention given by the government, healthcare in China will be improved although there may be more effective and economical ways to achieve the same objective.

8 Old Age and Unemployment Insurance

The government has also dealt with two other aspects of social welfare for the urban population which were previously provided by the state-owned enterprises. Since the late 1990s, it has set up step-by-step a nationally unified social security system for the urban population and has provided social insurance funds for this system.

In 1997, a uniform basic old-age insurance system for enterprise employees was established. It was financed by 20 percent of the enterprise wage bill and 8 percent of the employee's wage. A part of the premiums from enterprises go to mutual assistance funds and the rest to personal accounts. The premiums from the employees go entirely to personal accounts that belong to the employees themselves and can be inherited. This program expanded rapidly as the number of participating employees increased from 87 million in late 1997 to 108 million at the end of 2001, while the number receiving pensions increased from 25 million to 33.81 million. The average monthly basic pension per person increased from 430 yuan to 556 yuan. The rural population pay their own insurance premiums and withdraw funds from personal accounts with subsidies from the government.

In 1999, an unemployment insurance system was introduced. It was financed by 2 percent of the wage bill paid by employers and 1 percent paid by employees. Unemployment insurance benefits are lower than the minimum wage but higher than the minimum living allowance guaranteed for all laid-off workers. The period for drawing insurance depends on the length of the period in which insurance payments have been made, with 24 months as the maximum. The number of persons insured also increased rapidly, from 79 million in 1998 to 104 million in 2001.

In additional to contributions by employers and employees, the government has contributed a substantial amount. In 2001 it allocated 98 billion yuan for social security payments, over five times the amount in 1998. In 2001 the national government also established the Social Security Fund (SSF) as a national pension fund. At the end of 2008 the SSF had total assets of 562 billion yuan, an increase of 123 billion yuan from 2007, in spite of some losses in its investments in 2008.

9 Energy and Environment

Finally, there is the problem of energy and environment which the Chinese government has to deal with. There are four aspects of the energy-environment problem, namely (1) air pollution, (2) water pollution, (3) the emission of CO_2 in the atmosphere that causes global warming, mainly from the burning of coal, and (4) a shortage in future energy supply that relies on exhaustible resources. Environmental pollution from coal combustion is damaging human health, air and water quality, agriculture and ultimately the economy. China is facing all four problems. According to a report of the World Health Organization (WHO) in 1998, of the ten most polluted cities in the world, seven were found in China.

As early as 1979, China passed the Environmental Protection Law for Trial Implementation. The 1982 Constitution included important environmental protection provisions. Based on these provisions, the People's Congress has enacted the Water Pollution Prevention and Control Law of 1984, the Air Pollution Prevention and Control Law of 1987, the Water and Soil Conservation Law of 1991, the Solid Waste Law of 1995, the Energy Conservation Law of 1997 and adopted several important international agreements including the Kyoto and Montreal Protocols. The State Environmental Protection Administration (SEPA) was established in 1998 and upgraded to a ministry in 2008. However, enforcement of environmental protection laws is difficult because local government officials concerned with economic growth often do not cooperate. The 11th Five-Year Plan of 2006–2010 includes a target of reducing energy use per unit of output by 4 percentage points per year, but only 1.23 percentage points were achieved in 2006. China is also developing clean energy, including solar, wind, hydro and nuclear energy. Like other developing countries, China is going through a stage when the environment is damaged to speed up growth. As the Chinese people get richer, they will demand and can afford a cleaner environment. There will also be important technological innovations to enable the use of clean energy.

On the policy of CO_2 emissions, China as a developing country is paying less attention to that than to air and water pollution because the harmful effects of the emissions is not immediately felt. President Hu Jintao has stated repeatedly that China will bear its share of the responsibility to limit CO_2 emissions. A reasonable proposal for defining China's share of responsibility, as I have suggested, is to have the General Assembly of the United Nations decide on the total amount of emissions allowed each year or each short period and distribute the amount among the member nations in the form of emission permits. The permits can be freely traded among nations. To decide on the total amount, the General Assembly takes the median of the desired amounts submitted by its member nations. The corresponding number of emission permits will be distributed to its member nations in proportion to population. If we accept the reasonable assumption that all citizens in the world have an equal right to the atmosphere, each citizen is entitled to an equal share of the emission rights. Under this proposal, countries like the US which emit more carbon per capita would need to purchase permits from developing countries like China. China should have no trouble accepting its share of responsibility under this proposal because its carbon emission per capita is still low by world standards. The US can easily afford purchasing sufficient emission permits to allow its economy to function properly.

To summarize the prospects of solving the above economic problems in the future, poverty will be reduced but income inequality will remain substantial for a long time. Corruption will remain a serious problem. There will be improvement in the provision of healthcare and of old age and unemployment benefits. The environmental problem will be under control. None of these problems will be serious enough to generate the kind of political instability that will prevent the continued economic growth of the Chinese economy.

10 Prospects

Although the government has repeatedly emphasized continued economic reform in its Five-Year Plans, institutional reform will not take place at a rapid rate because officials in power and citizens benefiting from the current economic system would not like to see rapid institutional changes. In fact, China's moderation in reforming its economic institutions in the course of globalization has benefited its economy. Refusing to allow the free movement of financial capital helped China avoid the Asian financial crisis of 1997–98. Slow adoption of the use of financial derivatives and more regulation of financial institutions prevented extremely risky investments from taking place and freed China from the current world financial crisis. Of course, the world recession has affected China by reducing its exports. China will continue to take a cautious attitude toward the reform of its financial institutions. Because of the authority of the Communist Party and the State Council, China is able to introduce an effective set of government expenditures amounting to 4 trillion RMB in two years. This will offset the negative effect of export reduction and China will emerge from the economic slowdown earlier than other countries.

In spite of the slow pace of institutional reform, China will continue to experience substantial economic growth in the future. Economic growth will continue simply because the three economic fundamentals will remain in effect. The rate of growth will decline gradually because China is narrowing the gap between its stage of development and that of the most developed countries. I made a projection in 2001 that by 2020 the Chinese economy would surpass the US economy in total output. This projection remains valid, using more up-to-date information. In 2007, the US GDP was 13.8 trillion dollars. By its revised measure of purchasing power parity, the World Bank estimated China's GDP in 2007 to be 7.1 trillion US dollars, slightly more than half of the US GDP. If we assume the US GDP grows at 2.8 percent per year from 2007 to 2020, in 2020, the US GDP will be 19.76 trillion 2007 dollars. If China's GDP is assumed to grow at 8.2 percent per year, in 2020 it will be 19.78 trillion 2007 dollars, just slightly above the US GDP. The assumptions that the US GDP will grow by no more than 2.8 percent per year and that the Chinese GDP will grow at least 8.2 percent per year appear reasonable. In 2008, the US GDP had a negative growth, and even in years before the current economic downturn its growth rate was only about 2.8 percent. On the other hand, 8.2 percent is a reasonable estimate of China's GDP growth rate from 2007 to 2020.

In what form will this growth manifest itself? First, China's science and technology will advance to be at the cutting edge of the world. This includes information technology and biotechnology in particular. The quality of scientists and scientific research will improve because the government has a policy to encourage and support scientific research and the Chinese scientists are able and hardworking. Together with the improvement of science and technology, the quality of education at all levels will also improve.

Second, art and cultural activities will flourish. These come with economic development and are built upon the Chinese artistic cultural tradition. Today, young Chinese artists are already among the most prominent in the world. Their paintings command very high prices in the world market and works of well-known Chinese artists are exhibited in top art museums. The only question is to what extent traditional Chinese art will remain or will be integrated into the flourishing contemporary Chinese art.

Third, technological advances and increases in wealth will enable China to become a major investor abroad. China will provide capital and technology for many developing countries in Asia, Latin America and Africa. Its investment abroad has already expanded at a very rapid rate in recent years (over 20 percent per year in 2003–2007).

Fourth, along with its economic influence, China's political influence will expand and it will become a leader in the world political community. Much credit for this development goes to the Chinese government. It deals with other countries in a friendly manner, treating all countries as equal. It respects the viewpoints of other nations and does not impose its view on others. It is willing to help when help is needed. Therefore the Chinese government has made friends and influenced many nations. Its position in the world community will continue to rise.

I cannot end this essay without commenting on the possible development of democracy in China. If we read the annual Work Report of the Premier to the National People's Congress, we will always find a section on the progress towards the development of a democratic government although the meaning of democracy may not be shared by some readers. As the Chinese people have more economic power in the course of economic development, they will gain more political power, some by joining the Communist Party. Both economic and political freedom will increase gradually as it has in the past two decades. However, the one-party rule is likely to continue for some time to come.

Many western observers still do not appreciate the peaceful rise of China. Some fail to realize how much China has developed socially and economically. This misunderstanding has been partly corrected by the 2008 Olympics in Beijing and partly by personal visits to China for those who had the opportunity to do so. Others consider the rise of China as a threat. The misunderstanding will gradually disappear and China's position in the world will be further enhanced as I have explained. Residents of Hong Kong will continue to contribute to and share the fruits of China's economic development. Perhaps the residents of Taiwan would be proud to be a Chinese one day in the future.

4

How has the Chinese Government Changed Since the 1980s?

The Chinese edition of this book includes as the third article an interview by a reporter who asked me various questions. The question of most interest is in what way the Chinese government has changed since the 1980s. Here is my reply.

Time has changed. The spirit and attitude of the Chinese government officials have changed. In the 1980s many officials in the Chinese government were eager to serve the country. They realized that China was poor and wanted to improve China. They could act quickly when they saw an opportunity to move China forward. Let me give one example. In June 1984, after completing a workshop to teach microeconomics at Peking University to a selected group of young teachers under the sponsorship of the Ministry of Education, while on a train ride from Shanghai to Hengzhou, I thought of the idea of cooperating with the Ministry to select the best students in China to receive graduate training in economics in the United States and Canada. I immediately sent a telegram (no email at the time) to the Bureau Chief in charge of foreign affairs of the Ministry, with whom I had cooperated to organize the microeconomics workshop, to present this proposal and suggested that he could reply to me at Zhongshan University, my next stop. Three days later I did get a reply from him at Zhongshan University expressing his agreement. By September the Ministry was already setting up national examinations to select graduate students. Those who passed the examinations were recommended to selected universities at the end of 1984 and started their graduate studies towards a PhD degree in the fall of 1985.

Such prompt and decisive actions by Chinese government officials cannot be expected to happen today. China is much richer. Officials are less eager to take decisive actions because there is a risk of rocking the boat. It is natural that officials would like to hold on to their comfortable positions. Their behavior has become more bureaucratic. It is more difficult to suggest new ideas for them to act on, even if they believe that the idea may be good for China.

5

Why China's Economy has Grown so Rapidly

People wonder why China's economy has developed so rapidly in the last 30 years and consider the development a miracle. I do not consider this rapid development to be a miracle. It is rather the result of an economic law. Three important fundamental driving forces have been behind this rapid development. These are the same driving forces that contributed to the rapid economic development of Japan before and after World War II, and of the Four Dragons (Hong Kong, Singapore, Taiwan and S. Korea) from the 1960s to the 1980s. The factors are human capital of high quality, a set of functioning market institutions and being at an early stage of economic development which gives the economy much room to catch up. Let me elaborate on these factors in turn.

1. Human capital means the ability of human beings in the society, including the skill and work ethic of the labor force and the ingenuity and resourcefulness of the entrepreneurs. The quality of human capital is a part of a society's historical and cultural tradition and not something that can be installed in one or two decades. Economists have been accustomed to measuring the amount of human capital by the number of years of

schooling of the people. This measure is inaccurate because it fails to incorporate the work ethic and ingenuity of people that are the result of cultural tradition. These qualities are retained and improved from generation to generation and partly transferred through family education.

In China we can see the skill of the workers in ancient bronze vessels, embroidered silk, chinaware and Ming furniture, not to mention the Qin terracotta soldiers and armament in Xi'an. China certainly has high-quality human capital. Other countries such as Japan, Germany, South Korea, Singapore and the United States also have high-quality human capital, though of a different kind. A main reason why some countries fail to achieve rapid economic development is the lack of human capital.

2. The second driving force is the existence of a set of functioning market institutions. China had the same human capital before the economic reform started in 1978 but did not have market institutions. Therefore it failed to develop rapidly. Market institutions allow the talented people to better themselves by hard work, thereby increasing wealth for themselves and at the same time for the society. Market institutions allow economic activities to be well-motivated because hard work pays and to be well-coordinated because resources are channeled to where they are needed most through the market forces of demand and supply.

   The Chinese government deserves credit for changing the economic institutions step-by-step from a planned economy to a market economy. I have documented this transformation in my book *China's Economic Transformation* (Blackwell, 2004 and 2007) with the Chinese translation 中国经济转型 published by Renmin University Press (2005). However, market institutions without China's human capital could not have led to such rapid economic development.

   Some people have pointed out the many shortcomings of China's market institutions such as the banking system and the legal system. These institutions have been improved continuously. It is important to note that an economy can develop rapidly even when its market institutions are imperfect, as demonstrated by China's historical experience of the last 30 years. Furthermore, economic institutions themselves can be improved and developed in a market economy even without government action. In China, an outstanding example is the development of the township and village enterprises in the 1980s which sprang up to serve the economic needs of the time. Market institutions can generate other market institutions. The New York Stock Exchange today and the Shanghai Stock Exchange in the 1930s were created without government action.

One aspect of the interaction between human capital and market institutions is worth mentioning. The market system functions better if each person has an equal opportunity to compete in the market so that the more able will succeed. Equal opportunity is often not achieved in a mature market economy because the children of the successful have better opportunities. In 1978 when economic reform first started, most of the Chinese people had almost equal opportunities. They all started being poor and no one had inherited any wealth to start a private business when such opportunities opened up, although Communist Party members had better opportunities to run state enterprises and start private and village enterprises. At that time all students had equal opportunities to go to college or graduate school and the more able and more hardworking were selected to enter college or graduate school. I helped a number of excellent graduate students in the 1980s to enter graduate school in North America and many had come from poor and rural families.

3. The third factor contributing to rapid economic growth is the gap between the technology of a developing country and that of the most advanced countries. This enables the developing countries to catch up quickly by adopting the most advanced technologies.

Understanding these three factors, we can predict that the Chinese economy will continue to grow because these three driving forces will be present, assuming sufficient political stability. When the technological gap narrows, the rate of growth will gradually decline but the growth rate will be above 8 percent per year at least for another 10 to 15 years.

According to Professor Robert Fogel of the University of Chicago, in his speech given in July, (1) the rapid buildup of advanced technology, (2) a shift of labor from low to high productivity sectors and (3) investment in human capital were the three main factors that have enabled China to continue double-digit economic growth for more than 25 years. These factors are different from the three factors I have proposed. From my perspective, Fogel did not give the three main factors for, but only the three manifestations of, China's rapid growth. On (1) the rapid buildup of advanced technology, why have other developing countries not been able to do the same? To me the reason is that the Chinese human capital has enabled China to absorb modern technology and attract foreign investment which could have gone elsewhere. On (2) the shift of labor from low to high productivity sectors, this is a natural phenomenon of market institutions which also have other features favorable to development, such as profit motives for entrepreneurs to strive and incentives for individuals to invest in human capital. On (3) the investment in human capital, it is partly the result of market institutions as just pointed out. Furthermore, its quantitative contribution to China's GDP growth is questionable (and deserves careful study). First, observe that China was able to grow rapidly from 1979 to 1985 when its workforce had only limited schooling during the period of the Cultural Revolution of 1967–1977. Second, the education level of the Chinese working population increased only very slowly from 1979 to 2000, even allowing for the great expansion of expenditures on higher education since the late 1990s, because investment in human capital is only an increment of the total stock of human capital. Vogel later has pointed out to me that he was using the term "three factors" differently, in the sense of growth accounting in the framework of an aggregate production function.

6

China's History and its Human Capital

In a previous article I suggested that China's high-quality human capital is one of the three major factors accounting for its rapid economic growth (the other two being its market institutions and its low level of technology), and that human capital is derived from the historical and cultural tradition and not something that can be acquired in just one or two decades. The high-quality human capital is demonstrated by the opening and closing ceremonies and other aspects of the 2008 Olympics. In this essay I would like to elaborate on the historical background of China's human capital by going through the main periods or dynasties of Chinese history and illustrating how each has contributed to China's human capital today. Human capital includes the qualities and skill of the Chinese workers, entrepreneurs and researchers, as well as their attitudes and characteristics.

1 Shang, 1600 BC

Shang is responsible for the bronze vessels displayed in museums which show its advanced technology, mature culture and the skill of the labor force.

2 Zhou, 1100 BC

Zhou was a golden period in the development of Chinese thought, including Confucianism, Daoism and Legalism. Confucianism has given us the moral characteristics of honesty, hard work, loyalty to friends, respect for elders and respect for learning and scholarship.

3 Qin, 200 BC

The first Emperor of Qin unified China, including its language and measures, and established a system of central, provincial and local governments which has lasted until today. The dynasty shows an ability to build physical infrastructure projects including the Great Wall. It had advanced skills and technology as shown in the making of terracotta soldiers in Xi'an and of ammunition shown in the Xi'an Museum.

4 Han, 206 BC–220 AD

The great historian Sima Qian understood the functioning of the market economy which already existed for him to write about.

> There must be farmers to produce food, men to extract the wealth of mountains and marshes, artisans to produce these things and merchants to circulate them. There is no need to wait for government orders: each man will play his part, doing his best to get what he desires. So cheap goods will go where they will fetch more, while expensive goods will make men search for cheap ones. When all work willingly at their trade, just as water flows ceaselessly downhill day and night, things will appear unsought and people will produce them without being asked. For clearly this accords with the Way and is in keeping with nature.

The above text shows the division of labor among different professions. People do their work without government direction. Everyone tries to do his best to get what he wants. In the language of modern economics, consumers maximize utility and managers maximize profits. The price system works as suppliers will sell goods where the price is the highest and purchasers will search for goods that are least expensive to satisfy the same need. Everyone performs his function willingly and unceasingly in a market economy as if guided by an "invisible hand." Is this not the manifestation of the law of supply and demand in economics?

5 Tang, 618–907

Tang saw the expansion of foreign trade through the Silk Route which had already existed in the Han dynasty. Foreign trade is important for economic development. It is one aspect of globalization as globalization includes movements of goods (foreign trade), capital, technology/knowledge (foreign investment) and people (migration of labor). Poetry writing flourished in the Tang dynasty and has served as an important cultural and leisure activity for the Chinese people until the present day. In addition, Buddhism was imported from India to China, and helped in the development of a pluralistic culture in China. The Chinese people do not believe in only one God or in absolute truth. For this reason they may be more tolerant of the beliefs of others and more pragmatic in their behavior. Chinese government officials were pragmatic in carrying out economic reform since 1978. Pragmatism has contributed to China's economic reform and development. The Chinese adopt anything that works.

6 Song, 960–1126

During the Song dynasty a market economy flourished. We can see it functioning in the famous painting *Qingming Festival along the river.* The painting depicts various economic activities in Kaifeng, the capital of Northern Song. China had a mature market economy but lacked the development in technology that propelled modern capitalism. Historians debate the reasons why modern technology did not develop in China especially when the Chinese had been responsible for the greatest inventions up to that time: the compass, gunpowder, paper and painting. Some historians explain that, under the Chinese imperial system, high social status and the accompanying financial reward were given to government officials and not to inventors. In addition, for an innovation to be profitable, the scale of production had to be large but people did not take the risk to engage in large-scale production because labor was plentiful and inexpensive.

7 Yuan, 1279

Every primary school student knows that Genghis Khan built an empire covering much of Europe. His grandson Hubilie conquered China and founded the Yuan Dynasty. The Han Chinese were content to live in their own territory and tried to protect themselves against invasions from the North. They did not have an expansionary history and preferred peaceful coexistence.

8 Ming, 1415

Ming is known for its overseas explorations led by Zheng He, recently described in the book by Menzies (2003) entitled *1421: The Year the Chinese Discovered the World.* In it, we learn about the remarkable size and the large number of ships in Zheng He's fleet, showing the wealth of China and the advanced shipbuilding technology at the time.

9 Qing, 1760–1911

Qing had very capable emperors in its early years but the government led by later emperors became very weak at a crucial time when China had to face the effects of Western imperialism. Since its defeat in the Opium War (1840–2), there were more unequal treaties and China became a semi-colonial country. Modernization became the main objective of the Chinese people and nationalism became a strong force influencing the behavior of the Chinese government and the mentality of the Chinese people. China today favors equal treatment of all nations, a position which has helped China to win friends in the community of nations.

10 Republic of China, 1911

Given the dissatisfaction with the Qing government, revolution was inevitable, although there was a difference of opinion as to whether a constitutional monarchy similar to the one in Great Britain or a democratic republic was more suitable for China. In the first decade of the Republic of China, there was only democracy in name and not in practice. The presidency changed hands frequently, based on military power, and members of Congress were replaced by new members supporting the president. Representatives in Congress followed the political wind to elect a president. (An excellent book on the Chinese history of that period is 三水梁燕孙先生年谱.) We learn two lessons from this period. First, the successful introduction of a democratic government is dependent on the country's cultural tradition. Second, in spite of the political instability in the 1920s and 1930s, China's economy continued to grow substantially because of China's human capital. Since 1978, China has had political stability. No wonder it has been able to grow more rapidly given the same human capital.

11 People's Republic of China, 1949–

China adopted central planning with the First Five-Year Plan introduced in 1953. During the period of central economic planning before 1978, planners learned the shortcomings of a planned economy and to appreciate the value of decentralized decision making. The lessons learned in the practice of central planning have helped the later development of the Chinese market economy, although other lessons have yet to be learned, including the provision of healthcare by people-operated (*minban*) hospitals as discussed in my previous article.

In the Chinese cultural tradition, "learning" is considered very important. The first Confucian classic is entitled "*Great Learning.*" The "*Three-word Essay*" required to be memorized by children includes, "If a man does not learn, he does not know the way." We can learn from what the learned people in history teach us through the books – in 1700 there were more books in China than the rest of the world combined. We can also learn from the people of today who have inherited the Chinese culture and human capital. We can learn (学) for the sake of enjoyment in the process of learning itself. As Confucius said, "Isn't it a pleasure to learn and relearn?" We can also use what we have learned for enjoyment and for improving our social and economic wellbeing.

7

China's GDP to Exceed the US GDP in 2020: A Re-estimation of the Forecast

The statement in the title of this article has often been quoted in China. It was first stated in the first edition of my book *China's Economic Transformation* (2002, pp. 102–3) (Chinese translation by Remin University Press, 2005). Let me examine this statement to see if it is still true today.

My projection was based on the World Bank report *Entering the 21st Century* (2000, Table 1, p. 230) which provided an estimate of China's GDP in 1998 in terms of purchasing power parity that was half of the US GDP. This means that we cannot convert Chinese GDP in RMB into US dollars simply by dividing it by the exchange rate, which in 1998 was 8.3 RMB per dollar. The purchasing power parity exchange rate is the amount of RMB required to purchase a given bundle of commodities which one US dollar can buy. This rate was about 2 according to the World Bank. By this calculation, a dinner in 1998 that cost 15 US dollars in a medium-price US restaurant would have cost about 30 RMB in a similar restaurant in China. The same calculations were made for other goods like clothing, transportation, housing, etc. We then average these price ratios to get the exchange rate of RMB in terms of purchasing power parity.

To make the GNP projection, I assumed that from 1998 to 2020 China's GDP would grow at an annual rate of 6 percent. This assumption was conservative in view of the fact that China's GDP from 1978 to 1998 had grown at an average rate of about 9.5 percent. From this assumption I calculated the value of China's GDP in 1998 US dollars in 2020. Given that the US GDP was twice as large as China's in 1998, I asked at what annual rate the US GDP needed to grow in order to equal the above estimated Chinese GDP in 2020. The answer was 2.9 percent. This was about the median of the rates of growth projected by American economists. Since my projection of Chinese GDP was conservative, I concluded that by 2020 China's GDP would be larger than or at least as large as the US GDP. This was the projection I gave in a lecture at Fudan University in 2003.

Seven years have passed since I made my projection in 2001 (the publication of a book usually taking over one year after it is submitted to the publisher). I now re-examine the projection based on the information available today. My former projection may have to be revised for two reasons. First, we know that from 1998 to 2007 China's GDP has been growing above 10 percent per year, much higher than the 6 percent assumed in my previous calculation. This requires my projection of the Chinese GDP in 2020 to be revised upwards. Second, two years ago the World Bank revised downward by over 30 percent the exchange rate of the RMB measured in purchasing power. This leads to a downward revision of my estimate of China's GDP in 2020. Would these two factors cancel out to preserve the validity of my projection?

To provide an up-to-date projection of China's GDP in 2020 as compared with the US GDP in terms of purchasing power, using data for 2007 I found that that the 2007 US GDP was 13.8 trillion dollars. By its revised measure of purchasing power parity, the World Bank estimated China's GDP in 2007 to be 7.1 trillion US dollars. Please note the ratio of about 2 to 1, similar to the ratio the World Bank provided for 1998. This is due to the revision of its estimate of purchasing power parity. Let us assume that the US GDP will grow at 2.8 percent per year from 2007 to 2020. In 2020, US GDP will be 19.76 trillion 2007 dollars. If China's GDP grows at 8.2 percent per year, in 2020 it will be 19.78 trillion 2007 dollars, just slightly above the US GDP. Anyone who believes that the US GDP will not grow more than 2.8 percent per year and that the Chinese GDP will grow at least 8.2 percent per year will come to the conclusion that by 2020 China's GDP will overtake the US GDP. In 2008 the US GDP had a negative growth, and even in years before the current economic downturn its growth rate was only about 2.8 percent. On the other hand, 8.2 percent is a reasonable estimate of China's GDP growth rate from now to 2020. In conclusion, my statement as given in the title of this article remains valid from the data available as of 2007.

What can we learn from the above forecasting exercise? Readers who believe that my forecast is reasonable would conclude that some economic events can be forecast. Even if someone disagrees with one of my two assumptions (US GDP growing at 2.8 percent per year and Chinese GDP growing at 8.2 percent per year from 2007, to 2020), he can substitute his assumptions to make a forecast that he believes is reliable. Of course, not all economic events can be forecast, such as the prices of stocks traded in the Shanghai or Shenzhen stock markets. As another example, in the US today no one can forecast when the current recession will end. Among those events that can be forecast are long-run trends as given in the example of this paper. If we are willing to start with known facts, including the GDP data for China and for the US in 2007 supplied by the World Bank in this example, and if we are able to make reasonable assumptions, GDP growth rates of 2.8 percent and 8.2 percent for the two countries respectively, we can arrive at a reasonable and reliable forecast. Whether we should accept a forecast that some well-known economist makes should not depend on the reputation of the economist, but on the validity of his reasoning. We should not accept statements in economics just because they are made by authorities, but should accept only statements that are based on reasoning that we judge to be valid.

8

From Receiving Foreign Investment to Investing Abroad

Foreign investment has contributed greatly to China's economic development. It has provided the needed physical and financial capital, technology, management skills, access to foreign markets and training of the Chinese labor force. It has also provided competition for the state-owned and other domestic enterprises, making them more efficient. However, foreign investment is not a fundamental factor contributing to China's rapid economic development. I have pointed out that there are three fundamental forces underlying China's economic growth. These are the high-quality and abundance of its human capital, a set of effectively functioning market institutions, and the gap between China's stage of development and that of the most developed countries which enables China to adopt the most advanced technology to catch up. Without these economic fundamentals, China would not have attracted such large amounts of foreign investment because foreign investors could have invested their money anywhere in the world. China had the ability to attract and to utilize such large amounts of foreign capital.

Now China has become an important investor for other countries. Let us examine the facts and try to explain why this is happening. According to *China Statistical Yearbook 2008*, Table 17–20, China's net overseas investments in 2006 and 2007 were respectively 17.634 and 26.506 billion US dollars (176.34 and 265.06 亿美元). To appreciate the rapid increase, note that the total accumulated net overseas investment at the end of 2007 was only 117.910.billion US dollars. Thus the amount invested in 2007 alone accounts for 22.5 percent of this total. Note also that China's foreign direct investments in 2006 and 2007 were respectively 63.021 and 74.768 billion US dollars. Hence its rate of increase is 18.6 percent, much smaller than the 50.3 percent for investments overseas. By 2007 the ratio of overseas investment to direct foreign investment was already 35.5 percent. From the trend described above, this ratio can be expected to increase continuously in the foreseeable future.

There are two reasons for the rapid increase in China's overseas investment. First, China has become much richer and can therefore afford to invest. In the meantime, China has accumulated a very large amount of foreign reserves, over 2 trillion US dollars as of April 2009. Much of this amount is invested in US Treasury bonds which yield a low rate of interest and have become risky because the US dollar may lose its value. Hence the Chinese government is under pressure to invest this money elsewhere, possibly as overseas investment. Second, the Chinese are now more capable of seizing investment opportunities abroad. They are more educated, more informed of investment opportunities worldwide, and have became more skillful in investing in foreign countries through experience and improved ability to use and manage human and nonhuman resources abroad. When I refer to the Chinese, I mean both the Chinese government officials and Chinese entrepreneurs. The government officials may have other motives than purely economic returns from the investment. The Chinese government has to protect the strategic interests of the nation, including the control of important resources abroad, and has a policy to help less developed countries in their economic development. In investing overseas, the Chinese nationals also receive assistance and cooperation from the overseas Chinese.

In summary, both the government and the private sector are now more able to take advantage of investment opportunities abroad. The Chinese government has the vision and foresight in seeing the economic and political opportunities in other countries. The Chinese entrepreneurs are intelligent in searching for investment opportunities. In addition the skillful and hardworking Chinese labor force can be employed abroad. The end result is not only to speed up the economic development of China but also to increase China's economic and political influence worldwide. China's economic influence is thus derived not only from a large amount of domestic output and export, but also from transfer of capital and technology abroad.

What are the trends of China's investment overseas? In terms of the region of the investment, in 2007, Asia received the largest amount of 16.593 billion US dollars, but 13.732 billion of this amount was invested in Hong Kong and most of this was reinvested elsewhere. From 2006 to 2007 there were significant increases in investment in Singapore from 132.2 to 397.7 million, in the Republic of Korea from 27.3 to 56.7 million and in Vietnam from 43.5 to 110.9 million. Investment in Europe in 2007 was a little larger than in North America (1.540 and 1.126 billion respectively) but it had increased much less rapidly (from 598 million and 258 million respectively). By the end of 2008, there were some 1,200 Chinese companies operating in the United States, employing some 7,300 local employees. In terms of sectors, over 90 percent of the investment in 2007 was accounted for by the five sectors of mining, manufacturing, transport, trade and business services. This shows that the Chinese investors have expertise in investing in all these major sectors.

In a previous article I have described the success of China in developing clean energy and in controlling air pollution. Here is another aspect of China's successful economic development. Such successful economic development will

lead to the peaceful rise of China. Probably there will be obstacles along the way because many people in the world object to economic globalization in general, some countries are practicing protectionism and some people in certain developed countries are concerned about the rise of China in particular. I believe, however, that Chinese investment overseas will continue to expand and the peaceful rise of China is inevitable.

9

From Learning to Innovating in Science, Technology and Education

In the previous article "From Receiving Foreign Investment to Investing Abroad", I discussed one aspect of China's rapid economic development. In this article I will discuss another, related aspect concerning China's science, technology and education: 从学习到发明创造 (From Learning to Innovating in Science, Technology and Education).

China's progress in advancing science, technology and higher education is as impressive as in its economic development. As in the case of economic development, it is moving from learning and importing knowledge to discovering and exporting knowledge. Important progress has been made almost every year.

Let me first cite some facts. In higher education, the number of full-time teachers, which had remained at about 400,000 from 1988 to 1998, increased from 407,000 in 1998 to 1,170,000 in 2007, or by about 13 percent per year. From 1998 to 2007, the number of graduate students going abroad to study increased from 72,508 to 418,612, or by 22 percent per year, and the number of such students graduating increased from 47,077 to 311,839, or by 22 percent per year. In terms of technological innovations, the following annual data from 2003 to 2007 are revealing (see *China Statistical Yearbook 2008*, Table 20–38). While the imports of high-tech products were 1193, 1613, 1977, 2473 and 2870 (in hundred million yuan) respectively, the exports of high-tech products increased even faster, at 1103, 1654, 2182, 2815 and 3478 respectively. In the meantime, the number of inventions were 37154, 49360, 53305, 57786 and 67948 respectively, increasing at a very rapid rate.

In the field of economics, the remarkable progress in introducing modern economics into the university curriculum began in the 1980s. Under the sponsorship of the State Education Commission and with financial assistance from the Ford Foundation, we established two graduate training centers in Renmin University from 1985 to 1995 and in Fudan University from 1988 to 1993 and invited distinguished economists from abroad to teach modern economics. With the cooperation of the State Education Commission I also established a program to send graduate students to pursue PhD degrees in economics in the US and Canada. These programs have resulted in several hundred PhD holders, with many working as leading economists in China and in North America. Some are taking leadership roles in guiding a few top schools of economics. These schools have the financial resources to pay salaries that are competitive in the world market and are able to recruit able junior faculty members at the annual meeting of the American Economic Association in January each year. Several of these schools are very good. Some of their faculty members are among the leading economists in the world.

In the natural sciences and engineering, China had devoted much resources before the economic reform started in 1978 and has since made serious attempts to upgrade the quality of teaching and research. An outstanding and well-known example is the research group in computer science led by Andrew Yao at Tsinghua University. Yao was recruited from Princeton University in 2004, indicating that China was able to attract a top scholar from a top university in the US. As I helped to organize a forum in Princeton University last year and one in Shanghai Jiaotong University this year to discuss the problems of energy, environment and economic policies facing China, I found that in the fields of energy and environmental science and engineering, China has top scholars who are world-class and are contributing to the advancement of their fields. China is also known to be outstanding in other fields of the natural sciences. In physics the well-known program created by Tsung-Dao Lee to place graduate students from China to study in American universities lasted from 1979 to 1989, producing a number of outstanding physicists, some of whom are teaching in China.

What are the secrets of China's success? First, government policy and financial resources: The government has had a policy to promote science and education for the betterment of the China, and now it has the financial resources to achieve this goal. Expenditures on education and especially on higher education have increased tremendously since the later part of the 1990s. The main reason for the increase is that the government was able to collect a higher fraction of the GDP as its revenue when the GDP was growing at close to 10 percent per year. The government also decided to spend a much larger amount on higher education than before, as the above statistics show. The spending has been concentrated in a small number of leading institutions. The expansion of college enrollment was phenomenal in the late 1990s. Thus the government has the will and resources to push development in economics and in science and technology forward.

Second, Chinese talents: There are many able people in China and returning from abroad who can provide leadership in research and in the improvement of the top academic and research institutions. Many of these people are leading the development of the top institutions. On the financial side, leaders in society who have the foresight and financial resources are helping develop new centers of excellence.

Third, 制度: Although Chinese institutions are bureaucratic and some of their rules are rigid, some leaders in academic institutions are given flexibility. Some strong leaders can overcome bureaucracy and have achieved success in spite of the shortcomings of the Chinese academic system.

Once a few centers of excellence are in operation, there will be a contagion effect. The successful experience of one higher education or research center will spread to other institutions. As we can safely predict, a golden age of China's economic and intellectual development is fast arriving if it is not here already.

10

How will the Chinese Society Continue to Improve?

In a previous essay I discussed whether economists could make forecasts accurately and pointed out that there are certain forecastable events. The first type includes events that follow the laws of economics. The second type consists of unique historical events but the factors affecting them can be listed and the way these factors affect the event can be analyzed. For those events that follow the laws of economics, we can construct econometric models for forecasting. For the second type, we can apply qualitative methods to forecasting. Today I attempt to make a forecast of the second type.

The progress of the Chinese economy in the last 30 years is well-recognized. Today I would like to discuss the progress of the Chinese society. In particular the two important questions are what progress means in a society and how the society will progress.

What is progress for a society? We call it progress if people in the society live and work happily as they themselves recognize that they are living and working happily. What are the factors that can contribute to the realization of these conditions?

First, the economic conditions have to be satisfactory. People living in poverty can hardly be happy. Having good health is a condition for the happiness of an individual, but my topic is the happiness of a society of individuals. There are two other conditions.

Second, there should be law and order in the society. People should be law-abiding and not violate laws for self-benefit at the expense of others. This condition is related to the conditions of the economy. In conditions of poverty, illegal behavior tends to increase. During the current economic slowdown in the world, there are more criminal activities. Behavior harmful to others can occur in different sectors of a society, including the government, enterprises and educational institutions.

Third, people should uphold high ethical standards in their willingness to serve others. If they work together to improve the society, social progress will be achieved better than if they work individually. In summary there will be social progress if economic conditions are favorable and people are not only law-abiding but are also willing to work for the progress of the society individually and cooperatively.

I can predict that the Chinese society will continue to improve because the above three conditions are satisfied. Both the government and the Chinese people have contributed to the development of these three conditions. Since 1978, the Chinese government has initiated economic reform and provided a set of market conditions that allow the people to strive to better themselves, making the whole economy richer. In the non-state sector, Chinese entrepreneurs have contributed to establishing and operating the thriving enterprises that account for a large segment of China's gross domestic product.

In the meantime the government has provided economic and social infrastructures to facilitate such undertakings. In terms of social infrastructure, the government has invested substantially in primary schools, secondary schools and higher education, leading to a rapid increase in the education level of the Chinese people and hence their productivity and ability to improve the society.

On the contribution of the Chinese people, we recognize that the quality of the Chinese people is high. Once given the opportunity, there are able Chinese citizens willing to improve the society. Some may consider my statement to be too optimistic. Many able people are concerned with promoting their self-interest and not the interest of the society. First, many although not all attempts to promote self-interest lead to an increase in the welfare of the society, as guided by the invisible hand described by Adam Smith. Furthermore, even if there are only a minority of able citizens willing to work for the good of society, social progress is the result of a small number of great movers. Their work would suffice to produce continued progress for the society because they provide the important ideas and move others to cooperate with them to promote the social good. This basic law has been demonstrated in the establishment and operation of business enterprises, in education and research institutions and in other social organizations. China has a sufficient number of such social leaders who can work towards social progress in the present economic and social environment.

Needless to say, the Chinese society is facing serious problems, including corruption, social discontent due to income inequality and social injustice, and criminal activities harmful to society. For example, there is widespread corruption in academic institutions while much progress in science and education is taking place. On balance, the forces working towards social progress are stronger. Therefore, the Chinese society will continue to improve as it has improved in the last two decades. If readers disagree, I welcome their critical comments and stand to be corrected.

Part 2

Economic Analysis

11

A First Lesson in Microeconomics: Demand for Education in China

This article and several that follow are based on my lectures delivered at the Wang Yanan Institute for Studies in Economics (WISE), Xiamen University. What can explain the large increase in the ratio of educational funding to GDP in China from 3.4 percent in 1997 to 5.21 percent in 2002? Estimating the demand function for education will provide an answer.

There are two major factors affecting the demand for a consumer good or service. These are real income per capita y and relative price p. A demand function is an equation explaining the quantity q demanded per capita by y and p. It may bc approximated by the equation $\ln q = c + a \ln y - b \ln p + u$ where ln stands for natural logarithm. a is the income elasticity of demand. It is the percentage change in q when y changes by one percent. Similarly, b is the price elasticity. We can use statistical data on q (measured by student enrollment), y and p to estimate these elasticities.

By adding $\ln p$ on both sides, the demand equation becomes $\ln(pq) = c + a \ln y + (1-b) \ln p + u$. This equation explains the expenditure on education per capita pq. Since we have data on education expenditure per capita and income per capita for different provinces, we have used them (for 2001) to estimate the income elasticity a in this equation. The result for China is $a = 0.42$ for expenditures on primary school education, 0.81 for secondary school education, 1.29 for higher education and 0.88 for all three levels of education combined. The reader may try to understand why the income elasticities for the three levels follow the observed order. Given income elasticity $a = 0.88$, we have used annual data from 1991 to 2002 to estimate the equation $(\ln q - a \ln y) = c - b \ln p + u$, yielding an estimate of b of 0.44.

Now we are able to explain why the ratio of education expenditure to GDP increased as observed. Subtracting $\ln y$ from both sides of the above equation for $\ln(pq)$ yields an equation explaining this ratio as $\ln(pq/y) = c + (a - 1) \ln y + (1 - b) \ln p + u$. From this equation we see that if income elasticity a is close to 1, the effect of the income term is small, and if b is much less than 1, as in our case equal to 0.44, the ratio will increase as the relative price of education increases. In recent years in China, income has increased rapidly. This has raised the demand curve for education upward or to the right. The magnitude of the increase is about 8.8 percent for a 10 percent increase in real income. In the meantime the supply curve for education could not move to the right nearly as quickly. The quantity of supply (or demand) is measured by student enrollment and depends on the quantity of education facilities such as the total number of teachers and the total amount of floor space in school buildings. The facilities cannot increase by more than 5 percent per year because doubling the number of new teachers or doubling the space provided by new buildings can only increase the total number of teachers or the total floor space by a small percentage. Thus, the slow increase in supply relative to the rapid increase in demand accounted for the rapid rise in the price of education in China, by an annual rate of 10.6 percent from 1991 to 2002. This price increase, together with the above equation, can explain the rapid increase in the ratio of educational funding to GDP in China from 3.4 percent in 1997 to 5.21 percent in 2002.

Among the ten conclusions of the study (coauthored with Shen Yan 沈艳 and published in *International Economic Journal*, June 2006) are:

First, although China's education system is under the direction of the government, it is guided by market forces to a large extent. The fraction of non-governmental education funding (defined as total spending minus government budgetary spending) has been increasing in recent years and rose to about 50 percent in 2002.

Third, while the government maintains an important role in many sectors in the economy, including the industrial, financial, transportation and communication, foreign trade as well as the education sectors, it has allowed and encouraged the development of non-governmental institutions in these sectors. It is often the latter that has been the driving force of economic growth and development in an environment of free entry and competition.

Fifth, the framework of demand analysis is applicable to explain the spending on education, with real income and relative price as the major explanatory variables.

Ninth, on the relation between income inequality and education inequality (respectively measured by the standard deviation of log(per capita income) and log(per capita education spending) across provinces), to the extent that the demand for education is affected by income, income inequality will be reflected in education inequality. For primary school and secondary school education, the degree of education inequality is less than the degree of income inequality, indicating that education opportunities tend to be more equal among families of different incomes. However, since factors other than income affect education expenditures as well, inequality in education spending can be larger than income inequality. This is the case for higher education, and to a lesser extent for aggregate education and for its government and non-government components.

12

Supply and Demand for Healthcare in China

This is the second lecture I gave at WISE, dealing with an important problem. Many people would be surprised to learn that the supply of healthcare per capita in China did not increase from 1995 to 2004. This was a period of rapid growth with the consumption of almost every good and service increasing rapidly because of the increase in demand resulting from the rapid increase in income. If the supply curve is positively sloping, increase in demand will surely lead to an increase in the quantity of output produced.

What is the evidence that the supply of healthcare services per capita did not increase? A comprehensive measure is the total expenditure on healthcare in constant prices or in real terms. It is obtained by dividing the expenditure in nominal terms by the price index of medical services (= 1.00 for 1995 and = 2.616 for 2003). Medical expenditure in 1995 prices was 2257.8 (100 million) yuan and in 2003 was only 2516.9. Adjusted for population increase, the quantity of health care provided per capita remained almost constant during this period. Data from *China Statistical Yearbook* also show that for the same period there was no increase in the number of medical doctors or in the number of hospital beds per 10,000 population.

As in the case of demand for education, I have used the nine annual observations from 1995 to 2003 to estimate the following demand equation:

$$1\text{n}\ q = -2.564(0.490) + 1.178(0.395)\ \ln y - 0.707(0.222)\ \ln p$$

Where q is the quantity of healthcare (measured in expenditure in 1995 yuan per capita), y is the disposable income per capita and p is the relative price of healthcare (the above price index divided by the consumer price index). Thus the estimate of income elasticity is 1.18 with a standard error of 0.39 and the estimate of price elasticity is 0.71 with a standard error of 0.22. In statistics nine observations are often not enough for estimating an equation with reasonable accuracy. However, if the theory fits the data well as in the present case, nine observations are enough. Imagine having even only four or five points that fall very closely along a straight line. They are sufficient to give an accurate estimate of the intercept and the slope of the line.

To find additional information on income elasticity, I have used data published in the *China Statistical Yearbook* on healthcare expenditure per capita in 2002 for five income groups (very low, low, medium, high and very high) and plotted log medical expenditure per capita against log disposable income per capita of the five groups. For the urban and rural families, the five points are very close to a straight line. Their slopes give 1.080 as the total expenditure elasticity of demand for urban residents (with a standard error of 0.023) and 1.003 for rural residents (with a standard error of 0.023 also). Their average 1.041 is an estimate of income elasticity of demand for healthcare from cross-section data of 2002. We combine this estimate with the annual time series data to arrive at an estimate of price elasticity of demand for healthcare. Taking 1.042 as the given income elasticity, I have obtained the following regression by using the nine time-series observations:

$$[\ln q - 1.042\ \ln y] = -0.633\ (0.047)\ \ln p - 2.733\ (0.034).$$

Thus the re-estimated price elasticity is 0.63, close to the previous estimate of 0.71.

Using the above demand equation and taking supply q and income y as given, we can estimate the price p from 1995 to 2003. I pointed out above that our healthcare price index increased from 1.000 in 1995 to 2.616 in 2003. Relative to the increase in CPI by a factor of 3.346/3.028 = 1.105, the relative price index p in 2003 is 2.616/1.105 = 2.367. To find the average annual exponential rate of growth in p we calculate (ln 2.367 – ln 1)/9 = 0.0957. Converted to percentage increase per year, it is exp(0.0957) = 1.10 or about 10 percent per year. Our demand equation is able to explain the rapid increase in the price of healthcare (看病贵) by the lack of increase in supply and the rapid increase in income, given an income elasticity of 1.04.

The explanation for the lack of increase in supply is in the public provision of healthcare. This subject is more fully discussed in my paper "An Economic Analysis of Heath Care in China," in Gordon G. Liu, Shufang Zhang and Zongyi Zhang, ed., *Investing in Human Capital for Economic Development in China*. Singapore: World Scientific, 2010. The solution is to allow and encourage private provision of healthcare to complete with public provision.

The above discussion deals with the supply of healthcare. On the demand side, an important issue is how to pay for it. Medical insurance becomes an important issue. The Chinese government has tried to increase healthcare insurance coverage for both the urban and the rural population, the latter in the form of CMS – collective medical system. In the meantime the government is also considering increasing subsidies to public hospitals. The expenditures allocated to increasing subsidies may be used more effectively by subsidizing medical insurance coverage. If a hospital serves the public well, it will automatically receive such subsidies from the patients who choose to go there.

13

Is the Price of Urban Housing in China Determined by Market Forces?

Ever since residential housing in urban China became commercialized in the late 1980s, the price of houses has increased rapidly from 408.18 yuan per square meter in 1987 to 3366.79 in 2006, or at an annual rate of 11.3 percent per year (see Table 1). Such price increases have been of great concern to the Chinese government and the Chinese people. At times the government attempted to regulate the housing market because it believed that the rise in prices was due to speculation. For example, purchasers of new houses were not allowed to resell them within two years without paying a penalty of 5% in the form of a business tax on the total transaction price. I would like to point out that the price of urban housing in China is determined mainly by the basic economic forces of demand and supply.

As in the cases of demand for education and for healthcare services discussed in the two previous articles, let us assume that the demand for urban housing q, measured by floor space per capita, depends on its relative price p and on per capita income y, approximated by the linear equation (1), and that the

Table 1. Time series data.

Time (Year)	Urban Residential Floor Space per Capita (m^2)	Commercial Residential Housing Sales Price	CPI Urban 1978 = 1	Urban per Capita Disposable Income	Building Materials Industry Price Index (1986 = 1)
1987	12.7	408.18	1.562	1002.1	1.056
1988	13.0	502.90	1.885	1180.2	1.198
1989	13.5	573.50	2.192	1373.9	1.480
1990	13.7	702.85	2.220	1510.2	1.474
1991	14.2	756.23	2.333	1700.6	1.564
1992	14.8	996.40	2.534	2026.6	1.738
1993	15.2	1208.23	2.942	2577.4	2.481
1994	15.7	1194.05	3.678	3496.2	2.670
1995	16.3	1508.86	4.296	4283.0	2.841
1996	17.0	1604.56	4.674	4838.9	2.963
1997	17.8	1789.80	4.819	5160.3	2.951
1998	18.7	1853.56	4.790	5425.1	2.851
1999	19.4	1857.02	4.728	5854.0	2.785
2000	20.3	1948.43	4.766	6280.0	2.774
2001	20.8	2016.75	4.799	6859.6	2.746
2002	22.8	2091.72	4.751	7702.8	2.685
2003	23.7	2359.50	4.794	8472.2	2.674
2004	25.0	2197.35	4.952	9421.6	2.768
2005	26.1	2548.61	5.031	10493.0	2.786
2006	27.1	3119.25	5.106	11759.5	2.838

supply q depends on price p and cost of construction c, approximated by linear equation (2).

$$\text{Demand equation: } q_t = b_0 + b_1 y_t + b_2 p_t + u_{1t} \tag{1}$$

$$\text{Supply equation: } q_t = c_0 + c_1 p_t + c_2 c_t + u_{2t} \tag{2}$$

Solving these equations for p yields equation (3):

$$p_t = r_{10} + r_{11}\, y_t + r_{12}\, c_t + v_{1t} \tag{3}$$

that determines the price of urban housing. We have used annual data from 1987 to 2006 to estimate this equation to yield

$$p = -131.939(92.075) + 0.245(0.017)\, y + 412.237(120.858)\, c \tag{4}$$

$$R^2/\text{s.e} = 0.944/27.143.$$

The numbers in parentheses are the standard errors of the corresponding coefficients. Note that the size of the coefficient depends on the unit of measurement for the dependent variable p and the two explanatory variables y and c. In Eq. (4), p is the relative price of commercial housing, y is annual per capita real income in 1000 yuan and c is construction cost obtained by dividing the building material price index of Table 1 by urban CPI. Hence the coefficient 0.245 means that for an increase of income by 1000 yuan, the price index would increase by 0.245 units, and similarly for the coefficient 412.237.

Figure 1 compares the actual price with the price p^* as predicted by the demand equation. It shows that the factors of demand and supply can explain the price of urban housing well.

We assume a partial adjustment process for the actual price of housing to adjust within a year by only a fraction to its equilibrium level p^* as determined by the reduced form price equation (3):

$$p_t - p_{t-1} = b\,(p^*_t - p_{t-1}). \tag{5}$$

After substituting the right-hand side of Eq. (3) for p^*_t, solving for p_t and estimating the resulting equation, we obtain

$$p_t = b\, p^*_t + (1 - b)p_{t-1} = b(r_{10} + r_{11}\, y_t + r_{12}\, c_t) + (1 - b)p_{t-1} \tag{6}$$

$$p_t - p_{t-1} = b\, p^*_t - b\, p_{t-1} = b(r_{10} + r_{11}\, y_t + r_{12}\, c_t) - bp_{t-1}. \tag{7}$$

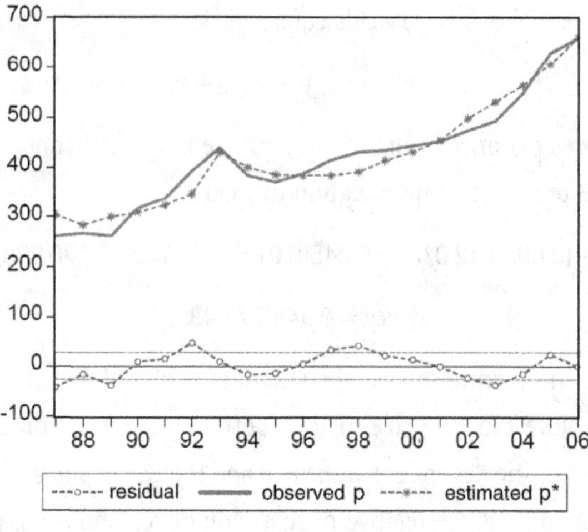

Fig. 1.

Then we can estimate the income and cost coefficients r_{11} and r_{12} in the reduced form price equation.

$$p - p_{-1} = -91.120(84.971) + 0.166(0.048)\, y + 283.413(132.592)\, c - 0.660(0.215)\, p_{-1} \qquad (8)$$

$$[-1.072] \qquad [3.424] \qquad [2.137] \qquad [-3.072]$$

$$R^2/\text{s.e} = 0.460/24.483$$

The actual change $p_t - p_{t-1}$ is plotted against its predicted value given by the right-hand side of Eq. (8) in Fig. 2. The result shows that our theory can predict the annual changes in urban housing price fairly well.

Returning to the demand equation (1) for urban housing, we have used time-series data from 1987 to 2006 to obtain

$$q = 9.854(0.943) + 0.01088(0.00097)\, y - 0.01039(0.00480)\, \hat{p} \qquad (9)$$

$$[10.449] \qquad [11.191] \qquad [-2.164]$$

$$\text{R}^2/\text{s.e} = 0.990/0.472.$$

An estimate of income elasticity is the coefficient 0.01088 of y multiplied by the mean 1191.539 of y and divided by the mean 18.39 of the dependent

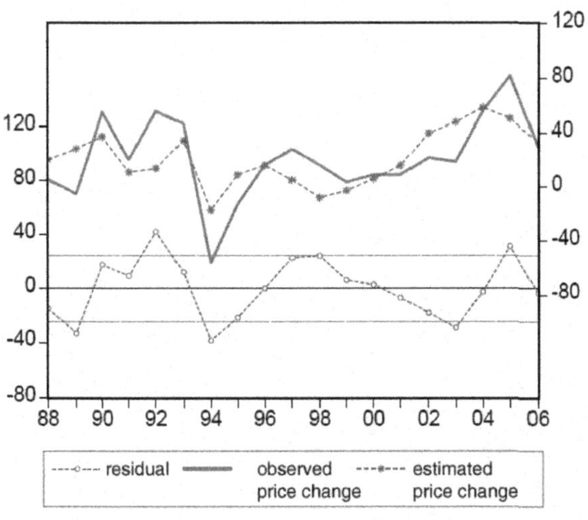

Fig. 2.

variable q, yielding 0.705. Similarly, an estimate of price elasticity is the coefficient –0.01039 multiplied by the mean 435.579 of $\hat{p}$ and divided by 18.39, yielding –0.246. The income elasticity is close to the estimate 0.940 for Beijing and 0.714 for Shanghai obtained by using data in the 1930s. (See *China's Economic Transformation*, Table 9.4.)

The above study (coauthored with Linlin Niu of WISE) shows that although speculation may have some influence, the basic economic determinants of demand and supply are sufficient to explain the variation in annual urban housing demand and housing prices in China from 1987 to 2006 at the aggregate level. If the past increases in the price of urban housing in China were the result mainly of increases in income and not of speculation, we can conclude that at present (although we have only studied data up to 2006), the theory of a housing bubble is not supported by the data and a collapse in the price of urban housing is not expected in the near future.

14

A Lesson in Macroeconomics: The Determination of Consumption and Investment

Economic behavior is the same in China as in other countries. This paper gives an example. Furthermore, good quantitative economic relations are valid for different periods in China, including both the periods of planning and after market reform.

In August 1985 I published an article in the *Journal of Political Economy* to explain how the two major components, consumption and investment, of real national income in China were determined in the period from 1953 to 1982. It turns out that the same theory is applicable to explain China's national income up to 2006, as I will show in this article.

About the determination of consumption, Keynes in the 1930s proposed that aggregate consumption increases with income but less than proportionally. If Keynes was right, economic growth in the form of an increase in income would lead to insufficient aggregate demand because (1) consumption would fail to catch up proportionally to purchase the increased output and (2) it would be necessary for the government to increase its expenditures to increase aggregate demand. Keynes turned out to be wrong in his pessimistic view (1) about consumption but was right to point out that (2) if there is insufficient aggregate demand, increasing government expenditures can help. Since the mid-1990s the Chinese government has subscribed to statement (2) of Keynes.

At the end of World War II, aggregate demand by the US government for military expenditure was drastically reduced. US economists and government officials were expecting a recession. However the US economy experienced rapid growth after WWII. This was the historical background for Prof Milton Friedman of the University of Chicago to challenge the Keynesian consumption function by advancing the permanent income hypothesis to explain consumption in 1957. He was later awarded a Nobel Prize for this piece of research. According to Friedman's permanent income hypothesis, consumption is proportional to permanent income; this proportion was equal to about 90 percent in the US at the time of his research and did not decrease as income increased. The reason is that consumers decide on the amount they consume according to their lifetime income or long-term purchasing power and not by the amount they happen to earn in the current year as measured by current income. Permanent income can explain the US consumption data much better than current income y. Later Robert Hall pointed out that if the permanent income hypothesis is correct, the best predictor of consumption in the next year is the consumption of the current year because it is proportional to or the best estimate of permanent income in the current year. Hence the amount of aggregate consumption in a year can be well explained by the amount in the preceding year.

To determine investment I assume that the desired capital stock is proportional to output. Since investment is the rate of change of capital stock (capital stock at the end of one year minus capital at the end of the preceding year), it is determined by the rate of change of output. This theory of investment is known as the principle of acceleration. Acceleration means the rate of change in speed and speed corresponds to the amount of output. When output keeps on increasing but the rate slows down, investment will decrease. Hence investment fluctuates more than output or income.

To summarize, the consumption is stable and fluctuates less than output; investment fluctuates more than output.

I have estimated the same two equations for consumption and investment using Chinese data from 1978 to 2006 as I did previously using data from 1953 to 1982. The variables are in constant prices. They are obtained by dividing consumption and investment in current prices by a price index. The results again confirm both the permanent income hypothesis of consumption and the acceleration principle of investment. In estimating the investment equation I used both the income of the current year and the income of the preceding year as explanatory variables. The coefficient of income of the preceding year turns out to be negative and equal in magnitude to the coefficient of income of the current year. This means the investment is explained by the rate of change in income as the acceleration principle predicts. I have found these two equations to be similar to the equations in my article published in 1985 using Chinese annual data from 1953 to 1982.

The theories of consumption and investment help us to understand the basic functioning of the Chinese macroeconomy. It is remarkable that the same theories of consumption and investment are applicable to China during the period of economic planning and after market reform up to the present.

15

Exchange Rate, Money Supply and the Overheating of the Chinese Macroeconomy

In my essay published in the February issue I pointed out that Milton Friedman had found economic theories that are universally applicable. Two examples are his permanent income hypothesis to explain consumption and his research on monetary theory and policy. I now give a third example relevant to China's macroeconomy today.

In the 1960s Friedman discovered that if an increase in money supply occurs, aggregate output of the economy will soon increase but the effect will be short-lived and prices will increase later but the effect will be long-lasting. This proposition came to my attention through a paper presented by Ben Bernanke, the current Chairman of the Board of Governors of the US Federal Reserve System, in a conference honoring Friedman in Dallas, Texas, in 2003. Bernanke conducted much research of his own using data for the US and other countries after Friedman's original research. After the Dallas conference, I decided to find out whether the proposition was true for China. At the beginning of my research Friedman was so confident as to say to me, "It will be true for China." After I completed a joint paper with Shen Yan (沈艳) of Peking

University on this topic, using Chinese data from 1952 to 2002, I found that the above Friedman proposition was indeed true for China based on data for the entire period!

One major cause of the "overheating" of the Chinese macroeconomy since 2002 was the continued rapid increase in money supply which caused a rapid increase in output year after year, according to the Friedman proposition. In 2000 and 2001, currency in circulation increased at an annual rate of 0.085 and 0.0683, and real GDP increased at 0.085 and 0.068, but in 2002 to 2005, currency increased at the rates of 0.0965, 0.1335, 0.836 and 0.1128 respectively while real GDP increased at 0.087, 0.096, 0.96 and 0.097 respectively. (Both M1 and M2 also increased at a higher rate in the latter period than in 2000–2001.) The delayed price increase is reflected in the inflation rates of 0.020, 0.020, 0.006, 0.0256, 0.0671 and 0.0380 in the years 2000 to 2005 respectively as measured by the GDP deflator (the price index that measures the average prices for all output included in GDP).

The rapid increase in money supply was the result of a large inflow of foreign exchange which was converted into RMB. In 2004 alone, China's foreign exchange reserve increased by 200 billion. By the end of 2006, total foreign exchange reserves reached 1,000 billion US dollars. When foreign exchange was converted into RMB, the People's Bank had difficulty controlling the increase in money supply with monetary policy such as increasing the interest rate and raising the ratio of required reserves to deposits in commercial banks. There was a construction boom which the government also tried to control by setting construction quotas. Such a policy was difficult to implement because the banks had so much money to lend out. If they did not have the extra money to lend out, there would have been no need to set limits on their lending or on the amount of construction.

The large inflow of foreign exchange was due to the low exchange rate of the RMB, making it cheap for foreigners to buy Chinese goods and to invest in

China. Given the current undervaluation of the RMB, foreign money will continue to flow in and be converted into Chinese money and the increase in money supply will cause a overheating in the Chinese macroeconomy. The officials at the People's Bank fully understand this problem but there are reasons, political and economic, for the government not to raise the value of the RMB rapidly to solve the overheating problem.

The exchange rate of the RMB was set too low as compared with the rate determined by the forces of demand and supply of US dollars in exchange for the Chinese RMB. The exchange rate in RMB per dollar is the price of the dollar. It was 8.3 RMB per dollar before July 2006. The higher the price of the US dollar, the less it will be demanded and the more it will be supplied. The inflow of dollars means that there are more dollars supplied than demanded at the existing exchange rate. This can happen only if the price of dollars is set too high, or the price of RMB is set too low. Hence an undervaluation of the RMB exists as long as there is a net excess supply of foreign exchange as evidenced by the inflow of foreign exchange into China. Only by increasing the exchange rate for the RMB will the inflow cease.

A country can adopt a fixed exchange rate system or a floating exchange system. A fixed exchange rate system is advocated by some economists for a developing country because under the system the monetary authority could not be irresponsible in printing too much money that would cost inflation. To maintain a fixed exchange rate with the dollar, the monetary authority cannot have a policy that causes too much inflation because inflation will lower the value of the home currency in terms of the dollar. Under a fixed exchange system, the monetary authority of the home country will give up its authority to carry out its monetary policy; its policy will be dependent on the monetary authority of the US. It cannot achieve a lower level of inflation than the level in the US even if the US is experiencing a fairly high level of inflation. For our discussion of the undervaluation of the RMB, there is no need to choose between a fixed or a flexible exchange rate system. China has adopted a managed floating system. Even if China were to adopt a fixed exchange system pegged to a basket of currencies, the evidence provided above suggests that the current exchange rate of the RMB is set too low and should be adjusted upward. Once it is adjusted upward to the equilibrium level, China can practice a fixed exchange rate system or a managed floating exchange rate system as it pleases.

Besides the undervaluation of the RMB, another reason for the construction boom is the public ownership of land in China. Government officials controlling land are tempted to approve the land for economic development during their tenure of office. When land is privately owned, as throughout Chinese history and in almost all other countries today, owners of land will not readily sell their land for construction because they may be able to sell it at a higher price in the future. Government officials can benefit from approving land for use in construction projects. Corruption will be the topic of a future essay.

16

Using Friedman's Theory to Explain Inflation and the Overheating of the Chinese Macroeconomy

Many people question the applicability of principles of modern economics developed and taught in Western nations to China's economy. These principles are applicable if one knows how to apply them. Knowing how to apply them is not easy. Hence many economists trained in North America and Europe may not be able to apply what they learned to the Chinese economy without sufficient experience.

To demonstrate the applicability of these principles, I use the study of inflation as an example. The quantity equation $Mv = PY$ is used to explain the price level P by the quantity of money in circulation M and real output Y, where v is velocity of circulation which is assumed to be constant in the short run. This equation was taught in Chinese textbooks before economic reform started in 1978. Written as $P = v(M/Y)$, this equation suggests that the most important variable explaining the price level P is the ratio M/Y.

In 1985 when I was organizing a workshop on macroeconomics in China under the sponsorship of the State Education Commission, I was asked by the Premier whether the sudden increase in currency in circulation (one measure of M) in

1984 by as much as 50 percent would cause inflation in 1985. I used the data from 1952 to 1984 to explain inflation (measured by the change in *P*) by the changes of (*M*/*Y*) and past inflation (because of inertia or delay effects) and estimated an equation to explain inflation. The result is that the inflation rate in 1985 was unlikely to be over 9 percent, which turned out to be correct. The reason is that the rapid change in *M* in only one year would not generate serious inflation. However, when the increase in *M* occurred year after year from 1984 to 1989, serious inflation did occur in 1989. This equation was updated several times after I first estimated it in 1985. My last study in 2006 showed that the same equation remained valid before and after 1978. Using the Chow test, I found that the equation estimated using data from 1952 to 1978 is the same as the equation estimated using data from 1979 to 2004 (see *China's Economic Transformation*, 2007, Chapter 6, and the article on the price level and output in the "document downloads" section of my website www.princeton.edu/~gchow). This is remarkable in view of the fact that for much of the first period, China was under central planning, and in much of the second period, China had a market economy. The econometric study shows the validity of this important economic law which is applicable to China and the rest of the world.

To extend this study that includes only one equation, I used a system of three equations to explain the changes in *M*, in *Y* and in *P* (inflation) by the past values of the same variables (see the above reference in my website). The relation between these variables are summarized by a proposition of Milton Friedman who discovered it in the 1960s. The proposition is that when *M* increases for reasons unrelated to the internal working of the economy (as summarized by these three equations), its effect on output *Y* will be almost immediate but short-lived, and its effect on the price level *P* will be delayed but long-lasting. Four years ago I tried to estimate these equations and to study the above two effects. Before my study (co-authored with

Shen Yan 沈艳 of Peking University), Friedman told me without looking at the Chinese data that my result would confirm his proposition, although at that time I was not certain that it would. Indeed, Friedman was right.

How is the Friedman proposition relevant to the topic of this essay? Since 2003, China's money supply was increasing rapidly, the result of which was an almost immediate increase in output *Y* but increase in the price level *P* was delayed until 2006. The rapid increase in output was called overheating. Besides the rapid increase in *M*, another cause of overheating was the rapid increase in construction when government officials in control of public land were eager to approve urban development projects when they were still in office. When I gave a lecture at the Bank of China in September 2005, I predicted that inflation would be forthcoming. My prediction was based on the Friedman proposition which had been shown to be valid for China. China's consumer price index rose 4.8 percent in 2007; as of July 2008 it was 6.3 percent higher than a year ago.

Why did the money supply increase so rapidly and can the People's Bank slow down the increase? The main reason for the rapid increase in the money supply is that the RMB was undervalued, leading to China having a large trade surplus and a large inflow of foreign exchange. The large inflow of foreign exchange was converted into RMB. It was so large that the Central Bank had difficulty sterilizing it. This uncontrollable increase in money supply will slow down once the exchange rate of the RMB is gradually adjusted upward to the equilibrium level in the next few years. Inflation will gradually slow down as well.

In the face of the current global financial crisis, China's economic growth has slowed down and the government has changed its policy from controlling inflation and overheating to stimulating output and employment, as I have discussed in a recent article in this column. China is better off than most other large economies. The negative force of reducing exports is not strong enough to cause a recession in China. It may not even be enough to reduce the growth rate to less than 7 percent because of the three major fundamental factors contributing to China's economic growth as discussed in a previous article.

17

Should China Revalue its RMB: Email Exchanges Between Gregory Chow and Ronald McKinnon

Email Exchange Set 1: Friday, July 29, 2005

Dear Ron,

A good friend Harvey Lam has sent me your article in the WSJ on the appreciation of the RMB which I have read with much interest. I happen to disagree with much of it and provide my comments below. Any reaction from you for my education and enlightenment would be much appreciated.

A copy of this is being sent to Al Harberger for his possible comments since he may tend to agree with you more.

Best regards,

Gregory

From the WSJ article by Ronald McKinnon with comments by Gregory in square brackets:

> On July 21, 2005, China again gave in to concerted foreign pressure – some of it no doubt well intentioned – to give up the fixed exchange rate it had

held and grown into over the course of a decade. Congress had threatened to pass (and may still do so) a bill that would impose an import tariff of 27.5% on Chinese imports unless the renminbi was appreciated, and had pressured the Bush administration to retain China's legal status as a "centrally planned" economy (despite its wide open character) so that other trade sanctions – such as anti-dumping duties – could be more easily imposed.

A decade ago, when negotiations over China's entry into the WTO began, a raft of Wall Street banks, investment banks, insurance companies, and other financial institutions subsequently pressured the U.S. Treasury to require China to loosen its capital controls and gradually permit the entry of foreign firms into China's domestic financial markets – even though these financial conditions were not required of other WTO member countries. China is complying with these terms, as well as eliminating tariffs and quotas on imports beyond what was required by the WTO agreement.

While (uncertain) currency appreciation or the premature dismantling of capital controls on currency inflows and outflows are not as malign as an opium plague, the danger to China's heretofore robust economic growth and great success in lifting large numbers of people out of abject poverty should not be underestimated.

[GC: There is no substantial causal relation between China's growth and a fixed exchange rate. Note that China's exchange rate v. the dollar was changed several time during this growth period.]

By holding the exchange rate of 8.28 yuan to the dollar constant for almost 10 years, and building monetary policy around this anchor, China's rate of inflation in its CPI has converged to that in the U.S., at a low level of about 2% per year. [GC: Here also, China had low inflation not because of the fixed exchange rate but because of the restrictive monetary policy of Zhu Rongji (low rate of growth of money supply) from 1996 to 2002.] In part because other East Asian countries (except Japan) were also more or less pegged to the dollar in a region where almost all trade is invoiced in dollars, the fixed dollar exchange rate was a very successful anchor for China's monetary policy. This collective dollar pegging within East Asia also ensured exchange stability and price-level alignment, which allowed regional trade and investment to grow rapidly and efficiently. Under the fixed rate, China's own high GDP and productivity growth were particularly impressive. [GC: No causal effect between the fixed exchange rate and GDP in the Chinese case, although for some developing countries which could not impose monetary discipline, a fixed exchange rate is good in forcing them to do so.]

However, on July 21, the renminbi was appreciated by 2% – a small amount in and of itself – while a narrow band of 0.3% on either side was maintained. More important was the implicit announcement that the old "parity" rate of 8.28 yuan per dollar was being abandoned, but there was no clear statement of how the heavily managed float would evolve. Now that the future exchange rate has become uncertain, executing monetary and foreign exchange policy in China will be much more difficult. I have five negative comments on the new policy:

(1) With the fixed exchange rate now unhinged, the People's Bank of China (PBC) will have to come up with a new anchor or rule that governs monetary policy. None was announced when the PBC let the exchange rate go. Will the PBC institute an internal inflation target? What will be the financial instruments it uses to achieve this target? [GC: If the People's Bank watches out for the growth of money supply, why would it need a new anchor?]

(2) Because China's inflation rate had converged to the American level (or slightly less), any substantial sustained appreciation of the RMB (the Americans want 20% to 25%) will drive China into deflation – preceded by a slowdown in exports, domestic investment, and GDP growth more generally. [GC: Substantial appreciation of the RMB will have an opposite effect: If we believe that rapid growth in money supply will cause inflation, then appreciation of the RMB will reduce trade surplus and the inflow for foreign reserves which have been turned into RMB to cause inflation in 2004–5. Appreciation of RMB will reduce inflation.]

(3) If the PBC allows only small appreciations (as with the 2% appreciation announced on July 21) with the threat of more appreciations to follow, then hot money inflows will accelerate. If China attempts further financial liberalization such as interest rate decontrol, open market interest rates in China will be forced toward zero as arbitrageurs bet on a higher future value of the RMB.

China is already very close to falling into a zero-interest liquidity trap much like Japan's – the short-term interbank rate in Shanghai has fallen toward 1%. In a zero-interest liquidity trap, the PBC (like the Bank of Japan before it) would become helpless to combat deflationary pressure. [GC: I agree with the speculative inflow of hot money due to small increases in the exchange rate, but the solution is to change the exchange rate by one big step, as China did in the 1980s up to the mid-1990s.]

(4) Any appreciations, whether large and discrete or small and step-by-step, will have no predictable effect on China's trade surplus. The slowdown in economic growth will reduce China's demand for imports even as exports fall so that the effect on its net trade balance is indeterminate. [GC: Ron, I must have failed my Econ 101 on foreign trade. I thought that increasing the value of RMB will make chinese goods more expensive abroad and foreign goods cheaper in China, both tending to reduce China's trade surplus. Of course the above depends on elasticities of demand for imports of Chinese goods abroad and of demand for foreign goods in China. Since there are substitutes the elasticities tend to be high.]

(5) Because the effect of appreciations on China's trade surplus will be ambiguous, American protectionists will come back again and again to complain that any appreciation is not big enough. So abandoning the "traditional" rate of 8.28 yuan per dollar will, at best, result in only a temporary relaxation of foreign pressure on China. [GC: This point might be valid.]

* * *

Lest you think that my assessment of China's new policy is too negative, compare it to the experience of Japan two decades ago and earlier. From the 1980s into the mid-1990s, Japan-bashing was in vogue in the U.S., much as China-bashing is in vogue today. Back then, Japan had the biggest bilateral trade surplus with the U.S. and was continually threatened (more by the Congress than the president) with trade sanctions unless there were temporary "voluntary" export restraints on particular exports, and the yen be allowed to appreciate. Indeed, the yen appreciated episodically all the way from 360 to the dollar in 1971 to touch 80 to the dollar in April 1995. This unhinged the Japanese financial system (the bubble economy of the late 1980s) and eventually resulted in Japan's unrelenting deflationary slump of the 1990s – its "lost" decade. Japan has yet to recover fully and remains today in a zero-interest liquidity trap, which prevents the Bank of Japan from reigniting economic growth. And Japan's trade surplus as a share of GNP has not been reduced in any obvious way. [GC: I do not know the case of Japan well enough to comment, but I will not easily accept the interpretation that the slowdown of the Japanese economy since 1991 is due to a flexible exchange rate. Anyone making such a statement has to document it carefully rather than just stating it. Perhaps you have written extensively on this but the above statement "This unhinged the Japanese financial system." alone has not convinced me.]

Thanks in large part to pressure from our lawmakers in Washington, China is now in a nebulous no man's land regarding its monetary and exchange rate policies. Instead of clear guidelines with a well-defined monetary anchor, its macroeconomic decision-making will be ad hoc and anybody's guess – as was (and still is) true for Japan. [GC: You may recall that I was one of the several economists who proposed a flexible exchange rate in Taiwan. After the Taiwan Government adopted the flexible exchange rate system the Taiwan economy continued to grow for a long period. The growth is now somewhat slower for other reasons.

Gregory

Mr McKinnon, a professor of economics at Stanford, is the author, most recently, of "Exchange Rates under the East Asian Dollar Standard: Living with Conflicted Virtue" (*MIT Press, 2005*).

Email Exchange Set 2: Monday, August 1 [Gregory's Comments in Square Brackets]

Dear Gregory:

Because you are truly the Dean of economists studying China, I am honored that you took the time to read my WSJ article and rebut it so carefully. The main difference between us is that I am a monetary economist who believes that, in an open economy, the exchange rate is just the expression of current or intended future monetary policies. But you are more in the mainstream in not taking this view.

I marked your main points in capital letters below, and am replying to each one.

(A), (B), and (C): In China's growth period of the 1980s, it was not a truly open economy. State trading companies for imports and exports insulated domestic relative prices from foreign – and of course exchange controls on both current and capital account predominated. Thus the Chinese authorities could change (depreciate) the official exchange rate (as they did several times) without having much effect on the domestic price level and monetary policy or growth rates.

However, by 1994, the economy had become much more open with the unification of the spot and swap foreign exchange markets and virtually accepting current account convertibility. The exchange rate made a big difference to the domestic price level, [GC: a questionable proposition, see below] and the over devaluation of the renminbi in 1994 when the official exchange rate and swap rates were unified at 8.7 yuan/dollar (the official rate moved from 5.5 to 8.7) greatly aggravated the inflation that had begun in 1993 and continued through 1995 [GC: also questionable, see below]. [GC: In my view (see "Money, Price Level and Output in the Chinese Macroeconomy" in the "document downloads" section of www.princeton.edu/~gchow and Section 7.3 of *China's Economic Transformation*) a major factor affecting the inflation rate in China is the rate of growth in money supply, M0, M1 or M2. In particular the inflation in 1993–5 can be explained by the rapid growth of currency in circulation, 317.9, 433.6, 586.5, and 728.8 (billion) at the end of 1991, 92, 93 and 94 respectively (see p. 120 of *China's Economic Transformation*). This happened essentially before the change in the exchange rate system in 1994. We disagree on the role of the exchange rate, as compared with the rate of growth of money supply, on inflation. I have documented my view about the importance of the rate of growth of money supply in the above two references.]

Subsequently, the PBC hung on to 8.28 yuan per dollar for 10 years through both deflationary and inflationary pressure until Sept 21, 2005. And in China's CPI price inflation in 2005, when the economy has become very open, has converged to being slightly less than that in the United States. I am not claiming that the exchange rate by itself anchored China's price level. Rather the government's use of some direct controls on investment, sterilization operations, and so on, were effectively guided by the exchange rate target.

Of course monetary cum exchange rate policy by itself affects mainly the rate of price inflation rather than the real rate of growth. However, I might note in passing that economy's rate of growth was more erratic from 1980 to 1995 – with serious inflations in 1988–89 and again in 1993–95. Since then, under the fixed exchange rate regime, growth has been very high, smoother, and without any significant inflationary outbursts. [GC: There is a short section "A brief monetary history of China" in "Money, Price Level and Output ..." to explain the historical facts in your last two paragraphs without resort to the exchange rate.]

(D) and (F): The rate of growth of the money supply as a target for monetary policy in the sense of Milton Friedman is just a non starter in a high growth developing country such as China. [GC: Nowhere do I express agreement with Friedman's viewpoint of targeting money supply. I do agree with Friedman's empirical proposition (pointed out to me by Ben Bernankee, who also agrees) that an exogenous change in money supply will increase output soon after but the effect will soon vanish and will raise prices with a longer delay but the effect is longer-lasting. To the extent that an undervalued RMB leads to more inflow of foreign exchange reserves (now of 700 billion dollars, with an increase of about 200 billion just in 2004 alone) which are converted to RMB, thus raising the rate of increase in money supply, the undervaluation is inflationary.] The rapid rate of financial of transformation and very high saving means that all monetary aggregates tend to grow explosively. For example, from 1995 to 2003 narrow money in China grew over 17 percent per year (See Table 2 of attached paper, "Exchange Rate or Wage Changes in International Adjustment?") and the broader aggregates grew even faster. [GC: 17 percent is not high for China for price stability from the viewpoint of the demand for money having an income elasticity over unity. Demand for money as the Chinese economy grows increases at a higher rate than GDP. The inflationary periods were those in which the rate of growth of money supply exceeded 25–30 percent – see table on p. 120 of *China's Economic Transformation*.] The monetary authority cannot simply "watch" the money supply and decide whether money growth is too fast or slow. Rather, it is better to treat growth in monetary aggregates as endogenous (not causal), and look for some other anchor to guide tightening or easing monetary policy. And for China over the past 10 years, the exchange rate has been the most convenient one, but now since July 21, it might have to move to domestic inflation targeting. [GC: In China, much of the growth of money supply (again see the above cited section of "A brief monetary history of China") was due to government policy, though not intended to control inflation. For example, currency in circulation increased by 50 percent in one year, 1984, because of the reform of the banking system when banks were given freedom to extend credits in ways not allowed before. Rapid increases of money supply in 1993–4 was the result of the banks loosening credit in response to Deng's call in his famous speech in Shenzhen in 1992 for further opening and rapid development. The success of Zhu Rongji in controlling inflation since the mid-1990s was by controlling bank credit and money supply using administrative means – imposing quotas on banks in each province. I am not advocating monetary targeting, but am pointing out that monetary aggregate is one of the variables that we should watch out for, including its rapid rise resulting from people converting dollars to RMB.]

(G): Because China's CPI inflation is now less than the American at around 2 percent per year, and virtually all goods traded in East Asia are dollar invoiced, a large appreciation of the RMB will drive China into actual deflation. [GC: A large appreciation will reduce the growth of money as compared with no appreciation. Actual deflation will depend on the growth of money itself which depends on other factors as well, such as those mentioned in the last paragraph.]

18

How are Prices of Stocks in China Determined?

Will the prices of stocks traded in the Shanghai stock market be higher tomorrow than they are today? This is a question economists cannot answer. However, economists can explain why stocks traded in the Shanghai stock market at the same time have different prices. This is the topic of the essay. As pointed out by economist John Williams, the objective of an investor investing in a stock is to obtain the future incomes to be derived from its ownership. The price of the stock should reflect the present value of its future dividends or returns. I would like to show that this theory applies to the stocks traded in China.

Based on the present value theory of stock prices and the assumption that the future stream of dividends can be summarized by the expected level of dividends of a stock in the coming year and the expected rate of change in this level, I was able to explain the prices of 17 stocks traded in the Hong Kong stock market which were included in the Hang Seng stock index as well as the prices of 30 stocks traded in the New York Stock Exchange which were included in the Dow Jones stock index (see Table 14.2 of my book *China's Economic*

Transformation). The evidence supports the conclusion that prices of stocks traded in mature stock markets can be explained by the present value theory.

In China the Shanghai Stock Exchange was established in November 1990 and stocks were traded in May 1992. Would the same theory be able to explain the prices traded in the Shanghai Stock Exchange? I tried to answer this question by studying 47 stocks traded in this market from 1993 to 1998 and found that the same formula based on the present value model was able to explain them equally well.

My formula was based on the assumption that the past dividends of a stock can be used to estimate the expected level of dividends in the coming year and the expected rate of change of dividends in the future, where the expected value is assumed to be formed under the hypothesis of adaptive expectations. The hypothesis of adaptive expectations states that the expected value of an economic variable will be changed in a period, say one year, by a fraction b of the difference between the observed value of the variable in the period and its expected value of the previous period. Let $d*(t)$ be the expected value of the dividend in period t and let $d(t)$ be the actual value of the dividend in period t. The hypothesis states that $d*(t) - d*(t-1) = b[d(t) - d*(t-1)]$. This hypothesis applies to the rate of growth of dividends also where the rate of growth is defined as $g(t) = d(t) - d(t-1)$.

Although the same theory applies to all three markets, my study has also uncovered differences in the relative importance of the expected rate of growth of dividends among the three markets. Investors in a mature market like New York consider the expected rate of growth as calculated by adaptive expectations to be more important in determining the price of a stock than investors in Shanghai. In other words, the observed rate of growth based on a short history is taken less seriously by Shanghai investors in calculating the expected present value of the future dividend stream for the determination of the price of a stock.

19

How are Stock Price Movements in the Shanghai and New York Stock Exchanges Related?

Today most observers agree that the Chinese economy and the world economy are integrated to a large extent because of economic globalization, but this was not the case in the 1990s. This essay reports on a study of the co-movements of the prices of stocks in Shanghai and in New York, as measured by the Shanghai Composite Index and the NYSE Composite Index. I use two variables to measure the weekly co-movements of these two price indices. The first is the rate of return, namely, the difference between the natural logs of the prices at the beginning of two adjacent weeks. The second, to measure the volatility in the rate of return, is the absolute value of the difference between the natural logs of prices at the beginning of two adjacent weeks. The variance of the rate of return is not used because it can often take extreme values, making the statistical results less robust. The data used cover 528 weeks, from the first week of 1992 to the eighth week of 2002.

By regressing the rate of return on its own lagged values for each market separately, I found that the efficient market hypothesis of stock prices is valid, namely, past values of the rate of return cannot be used to predict its future value. The mean rate of return in Shanghai and the volatility of the rate of return in Shanghai are both much higher than in New York. Most interestingly, the volatilities of these two markets are negatively correlated.

To be more specific, the mean weekly rates of return, when converted to annual rates, were 17.5 percent for Shanghai and only 9.5 percent for New York. This difference essentially remains when corrected by the rate of inflation since, during this period, China's mean annual inflation, rate was 5.3 percent and the US mean inflation rate was 2.6 percent. Adjusted for inflation, the real rate of return in Shanghai was 17.5 − 5.3 = 12.2 percent while the rate in New York was 9.5 − 2.6 = 6.9 percent. The difference may be explained by the much higher rate of economic growth in China while the Chinese stock market was somewhat isolated from the foreign investors who were allowed to buy only B shares that were traded separately.

On volatility, from 1992 to 2002, the mean of the absolute value of the rate of return was 0.01437 and the standard deviation of the rate of return was 0.00015 for New York; the respective figures were 0.04265 and 0.00304 for Shanghai. This may suggest that investing in Shanghai stocks was more risky during this period.

On the interesting negative relation between the volatility measures of the price indices in the two markets, we cannot conclude that they are related by any real economic factors. One interpretation of this phenomenon is that during this period the macroeconomic developments of the two countries happened to be different and stock price volatility is correlated with certain measures of the macroeconomy. During this period the correlation between annual GDP in the two countries happened to be negative. These two countries experienced different macroeconomic histories. In the US there was economic growth mainly driven by the technological improvements while in China political factors affected the rate of economic growth. Beginning with slower growth in the aftermath of the Tiananmen incident of 1989, China had a surge of economic activities stimulated by Deng Xiaoping's speech in 1992 during his Southern Expedition, followed by Zhu Rongji's effort to slow down inflation in the mid-1990s, the Asian financial crisis of 1997–99 and economic recovery afterwards. In any case, the growth rates of the macroeconomies of the two countries were negatively related. To the extent that factors affecting the volatilities of the rate of return in stock prices in the two countries are correlated with macroeconomic variables, measures of volatilities in the two countries can be negatively correlated as a result of spurious correlations.

As we have observed, the differences in both the rate of return and its volatility in the two markets were narrowing from 1992 to 2002. As this trend continues and as the Chinese economy becomes more integrated into the world economy, we can expect that a similar study using more recent data will show that the co-movements in the two stock price indices will be more synchronized than observed in this study.

20

Misunderstanding of China in the Western Press

Although people in the West have changed their view of the Chinese economy for the better, many still hold a negative opinion. In this paper I will give two examples. The first is from a top-rated economics journal in the United States. The second is from a top-rated economics magazine in the United Kingdom. Both publications have published high-quality articles in areas other than the Chinese economy.

In the December 2003 issue of the *Journal of Political Economy*, published by the University of Chicago, Alwyn Young wrote an article to express the viewpoint that statistics on GDP published in The *China Statistical Yearbook* are biased upward, to the point that in the 20-year period from 1978 to 1998, the annual rate of increase in China's real GDP should be reduced by about two percentage points per year, from 9.1 percent to 7.4 percent.

This alleged upward bias is very serious, to the point of being almost impossible. The Chinese National Bureau of Statistics may be able to overestimate the increase in China's GDP by two percentage points for one or two years but not by two percentage points for 20 years. Let the GDP figure in 1978 be

1 for normalization. To accumulate a two percentage point upward bias in the rate of increase, say from 8 percent to 10 percent per year for 20 years would make the estimate of the level of GDP in 1998 to be $(1.1)^{20}$ as compared with the true figure of $(1.08)^{20}$. It is a difference of between 6.7275 and 4.6610. The former biased estimate is 44.3 percent higher. How could the *China Statistical Yearbook* hide an overestimation of the level by 44.3 percent of the true figure?

Young (2003) also claims that the official estimate of the annual rate of growth of real GDP and of industrial output from 1978 to 1998 was about two percentage point too high. From *China Statistical Yearbook 1999*, Table 13–12, I have found data on the output of 23 products, including (a) nine consumer non-durables (chemical fiber, yarn, cloth, silk, paper and paper boards, sugar, vegetable oil, beer and cigarettes), (b) five consumer durables (refrigerators, electric fans, household washing machines, color television sets and cameras), (c) eight consumer and producer goods (electricity, hydropower, steel products, cement, plate glass, plastics, motor vehicles and trucks) and (d) construction, all in physical units. Using the outputs of group (a) and (b) combined, weighted by their prices in 1987 (as found in *China Commodity Prices Statistical Yearbook 1989*, pp. 175–6, supplemented by pp. 172–4), yields an exponential growth rate of 0.09129; group (c) provides a mean growth rate of 0.09356 and construction (d) grew in terms of completed floor space at a rate of 0.10364. Since (d) is 12.3 percent of industrial output, we take a weighted mean of the above three growth rates with the respective weights of 0.4385, 0.4385 and 0.123. The result is 0.094 as compared with the official growth rate of 0.112 for industrial output.

There are two sources of downward bias in my estimation of the growth rate of 0.094 for industrial output. First is the use of 1987 prices rather than the prices of earlier years as used in the official index, because earlier prices would give larger weights to consumer durables which have grown more rapidly.

Second, and more importantly, the method ignores the introduction of many new products during the 20 year period such as computers which have grown rapidly. Allowing for these two sources of underestimation would raise our estimate of 0.094 easily to 0.112 and contradicts Young's claim that the official growth rate of 0.112 is overestimated by about 2 percentage points.

Young's main point is that if we deflate nominal output by its implicit deflator to obtain real output, the estimated increase in real output is too large because the deflator underestimates the true inflation rate. By replacing the output deflator by another official price index for each of the three sectors, as given in his Table 3 (using the farm and sideline products purchasing price index for the primary sector, using the ex-factory industrial price index for the secondary sector and using the service price component of the consumer price index for the tertiary sector), the official growth rates of real GDP and of its non-agricultural components from 1978 to 1998 were reduced respectively from 0.091 and 0.106 to 0.074 and 0.081. The annual growth rates of real GDP according to the *CSY* estimate and alternative estimate are given in Fig. 2 of Young (2003).

The most dramatic difference between the official and Young's estimates of GDP growth occurs in 1989 when the latter estimate shows a negative 5.2 percent and the former shows a positive 4 percent. The negative growth is attributed (p. 1232) to "the forces that precipitated the political unrest of that year." This estimate does not seem plausible for at least two reasons. First, there was no sign of significant economic disruption in the first five months of the year. Peaceful demonstrations did not start until April and the Tiananmen incident occurred on June 4, 1989. According to the *CSY*, China's real GDP was growing at 11.3 percent in 1988 and a reduction to the official rate of 4.1 percent in 1989 was a very large one. We can reasonably assume that for the first six months of 1989, real GDP was increasing at least at 7 percent annually as compared with 11.3 percent the year before. To get a negative growth of −5.2 percent for the entire year would require an annual rate of decline in output of −17.4 percent ([7 − 17.4]/2 = −5.2) in the second half of 1989, which is highly unlikely. Even if we accept the adjusted rate of growth of 6.3 percent provided by Young for 1988 (as read from his Fig. 2) and assume annual growth of 4 percent in the first half of 1989, to arrive at a negative growth of −5.2 percent for the entire year would require an annual rate of decline of −14.4 percent in the second half of 1989, which is also highly unlikely.

The second example is an article in the *Economist*, which is as respected as a magazine for popular reading as the *Journal of Political Economy* is for professional economists. One morning I went to the lounge for the economics faculty and graduate students and picked up a copy of the December 11, 2008, issue of the *Economist*. On its cover was the title of its leading article: "Suddenly vulnerable: Asia's two big beasts are shivering. India's economy is weaker, but China's leaders have more to fear." I understand that China's economy had problems during the world recession but would not call China "a big beast shivering" or say "China's leaders have more to fear." Such statements alone show the bias of the article. I was very curious to find out what evidence the authors had to say such a thing about China, in order to learn more about the Chinese economy.

Let me quote the most serious, condemning statements and point out the absence of evidence supporting them:

> If China's growth rate were to fall to 5.5% or less, it would be regarded as a disaster at home and abroad.

Note the word "if" and the lack of supporting evidence.

> Yet in China, too, the present downturn is jangling nerves. The country is a statistical haze, but the trade figures for last month — with exports 2% lower than in November 2007 and imports 18% down — were shocking. Power generation, generally a reliable number, fell by 7%. Even though the World

> Bank and other forecasters still expect China's GDP to grow by 7.5% in 2009, that is below the 8% level regarded, almost superstitiously, as essential if huge social dislocation is to be avoided. Just this month a senior party researcher gave warning of what he called, in party-speak, "a reactive situation of mass-scale social turmoil". Indeed, demonstrations and protests, always common in China, are proliferating, as laid-off factory-workers join dispossessed farmers, environmental campaigners and victims of police harassment in taking to the streets.

These statements are only speculations and not hard evidence. Note also that the Word Bank's forecast of the growth rate of China's GDP is much higher than the authors', that power generation is not a reliable measure of output and that an 8% growth is essential to avoid huge social dislocation.

> Last month it announced a huge 4 trillion yuan (nearly $600 billion) fiscal-stimulus package. Some who have crunched the numbers argue that this was all mouth and no trousers – much of it made up by old budget commitments, double-counting and empty promises. It was thus mainly propaganda, to convince China's own people and the outside world that the government was serious about stimulating demand at home.

The following two paragraphs are only biased opinions and not based on economic analysis:

> In two respects, however, India has a big advantage over China in coping with an economic slowdown. It has all-too extensive experience in it; and it has a political system that can cope with disgruntlement without suffering existential doubts. India pays an economic price for its democracy. Decision-making is cumbersome. And as in China, unrest and even insurgency are widespread. But the political system has a resilience and flexibility that China's own leaders, it seems, believe they lack. They are worrying about how to cope with protests. India's have their eyes on a looming election.
>
> It used to be a platitude of Western – and Marxist – analysis of China that wrenching economic change would demand political reform. Yet China's economy boomed with little sign of any serious political liberalization to match the economic free-for-all. The cliché fell into disuse. Indeed, many, even in

democratic bastions such as India, began to fall for the Chinese Communist Party's argument that dictatorship was good for growth, whereas Indian democracy was a luxury paid for by the poor, in the indefinite extension of their poverty.

Reference

Young, Alwyn, "Gold into Base Metals: Productivity Growth in the People's Republic of China during the Reform Period," *Journal of Political Economy*, 111 (December 2003): 1220–1261.

21

Are Chinese Official Statistics Reliable?

1 Introduction

On the question raised in this paper, "Are Chinese official statistics reliable?" economists and general observers have different opinions. My view is that the statistics are by and large reliable and useful for drawing conclusions about the Chinese economy but some statistics are not reliable.

A general discussion of data quality is provided in Section 2. In Section 3 I will present evidence for the usefulness of official data by drawing from my own experience in using them to perform econometric analyses in order to understand the Chinese economy. In Section 4 I will cite some examples of errors in official statistics. Section 5 is an examination of possible errors in the official estimates of GDP growth. Although growth and inequality are two equally important topics in China's economic development today, I will not examine the quality of the data on income inequality because it is not considered a major issue in the discussion of data quality. This paper does not discuss data bias and data accuracy separately as it treats data bias as a special case of data quality. Section 6 concludes.

2 Data Quality in General

A most careful and systematic study on this subject is Holz (2005) which contains the following conclusions on data quality (p. 10):

> However one may evaluate the allegations of data falsification in certain years, even the critics acknowledge that long-run growth trends are approximately correct. The data problems reported here are facts which are unlikely to be unique to China; other transition and developing countries experience similar difficulties. The margins of errors are inevitably larger than in developed counties, perhaps even uncomfortably large...

I agree with the above assessment and also with the author's statement that "hard evidence [on data manipulation] is relatively scarce..." (p. 7).

This paper draws on my own experience in examining and using Chinese official data to update Chow (1986) and is supplementary to the careful study of Holz (2005) with which I essentially agree.

The evidence available to me has led to the following propositions:

A. The *China Statistical Yearbook* published annually since 1981 by the Chinese National Bureau of Statistics (formerly the State Statistics Bureau) is the product of its staff members located in Beijing and in various provinces and cities who are required by law to provide accurate statistics (Chow, 1986, Section 5, on the Law of Statistics passed by the National People's Congress (NPC) on December 8, 1983). Holz (2005, p. 22) updates this legal requirement when he writes: "The Statistics Law states that 'statistical personnel must seek truth from facts, strictly abide by professional standards, ... and leaders of localities, government departments, or other units may not order or ask statistical departments and statistical personnel to change or falsify statistical data.' (NPC, 15 May 1996, Art.

24 and 7). Yet the rule of law may have to defer to Party primacy." I will discuss possible political influence below.

B. Reports of the Chinese premier on the work of the government presented before the annual meetings of the Chinese National People's Congress are based on official statistics related to the accomplishments of the past year or to the annual plan (part of the Five-Year Plan) for the coming year. This shows that the statistics are used for internal planning purposes and are subject to review by all members of the National People's Congress and by international observers. There is no incentive for the Premier to lie not only because his report is under the scrutiny of the entire world but because using fabricated data would only lead to confusion of all government officials using such data for their work in economic planning and development.

C. Numerous scholars have used Chinese official data to perform econometric analyses that are published in professional journals and subject to the review of referees. This shows that most economists believe that the data used are reliable enough for drawing valid conclusions about the Chinese economy.

D. Errors in the data have been found, showing that some data are not reliable.

E. An obvious implication of propositions C and D is that one can use official data but should exercise caution to make sure that the data are reliable for the purpose at hand.

Proposition A is a statement of the mission of the people producing official statistics as required by law. It is a partial guarantee of honest reporting unless the staff members are not law-abiding.

Critics of propositions A and B might say that the staff of the National Statistics Bureau is somehow under pressure from the Premier or other officials of the

State Council to falsify statistics for political purposes. Proposition B asserts that both the Premier's office and the Statistics Bureau are under the scrutiny of the members of the National People's Congress and the entire world and that by using falsified data government officials cannot perform effectively their work in economic development. For the critics to be right, the Premier or one of the officials under him has to be dishonest in directing activities related to the Five-Year Plan, the Statistics Bureau has to be willing to assist the dishonest person by falsifying data and, finally, such cooperative deception has to go undetected by observers in the entire world. It appears to me that these three conditions are difficult to meet, although some critics may still cite examples of falsifying the rates of growth of GDP either upwards or downwards as a result of political pressure, a topic to which I will return below.

To respond to the critics of proposition B, I quote from Chow (2004, pp. 61–2):

> In more recent years, Premier Zhu Rongji announced targets for total national output and outputs of particular provinces in 1999, 2000, 2001 and 2002. A provincial governor might have been tempted to falsify data to fulfill the target stated by the Premier, but the staff of the State Statistical Bureau in Beijing had all the incentive to correct any falsified statistics reported from below. Premier Zhu would not have tolerated such false reporting and would have punished anyone responsible.

The National Bureau of Statistics also has staff in its branch offices in different provinces and cities to collect data and to check the accuracy of the data reported (see Holz, 2005, pp. 11–2).

To check whether the Bureau tended to publish output data to comply with the targets set by the Premier, consider the following annual growth rates of real GDP published in *China Statistical Yearbook 2004*, Table 3-3, except for 2004–5 which are based on an article on inflation in *China Daily*, July 21, 2005:

What evidence can the critics provide to claim that the official growth rates in 1998–2001 are overestimates? If they were overestimates, the Bureau would

Table 1. Annual growth rates of real GDP published in *China Statistical Yearbook 2004.*

Year	1996	1997	1998	1999	2000	2001	2002	2003	2004	2005
Growth	9.8	8.6	7.8	7.2	8.4	7.2	8.9	10.0	9.5	9.3

Source: China Statistical Yearbook 2004, Table 3-3.

have to lower the growth rates in later years to compensate for them since all output data are also reported in physical units which the readers can check independently. The Bureau did have a chance to under-report the growth rates after 2001 because the target growth rates were lower than the rates reported in Table 1.

The Outline for the 10th Five-Year Plan of the National Economic and Social Development of the People's Republic of China, passed by the National People's Congress on March 15, 2001, set a target for annual GDP growth in the period 2001–5 of "approximately 7 percent" and a target for the year 2005 at approximately 12.5 trillion yuan in 2000 prices (Chapter 2, paragraph 2). First, the official annual growth rates in 2001–5 were all above 7 percent and some much above. This shows that political pressure did not force the Bureau to comply and that if it had done so by overestimating the growth rates the years before, the Bureau could have reduced the growth rates in these later years to compensate and it did not. Second, applying the above growth rates from 2001 to 2005, we find that the real output in 2005 would be 1.537 times the output of 2000. Given a 2000 GDP of 8.95 trillion, the reported 2005 GDP in 2000 prices would be 13.76 trillion, exceeding the 12.5 trillion target by 10 percent. Thus the Statistics Bureau allowed an overestimation of the target by about 2 percentage points per year for five years. The growth targets might have been set conservatively to insure a high chance of being achieved, but the evidence of the Bureau reporting real output falsely in order to comply with announced targets is lacking from the above data.

The above discussion also points to the impossibility of fabricating incorrect growth rates for a long period. As pointed out in Chow (2004, pp. 59–60):

> For the purpose of studying long-term trends, we can tolerate sizable inaccuracies in the levels of the variables... To illustrate, according to official data, China's GDP was 362.4 billion (in constant 1978 yuan) in 1978 and 2312.9 billion in 1998. The exponential rate of growth in this 20-year period is [ln(2312.9) – ln(362.4)]/20 or 0.09268... Let both the 1978 and the 1998 GDP be overestimates, but the latter be an overestimate by as much as 30 percent more, relative to the former. We therefore should revise it downward from 2312.9 to 1779.2 billion yuan. The revised annual exponential rate of growth rate is [ln(1779.2) – ln(362.4)]/20 or 1.083 ... Thus even such a large relative error in the 1998 estimate does not alter the conclusion of a very rapid rate of growth. The reason is that when the estimate for the terminal year is reduced substantially, the effect is averaged out over 20 years in calculating the average rate of growth.

3 Using Official Statistics to Understand the Chinese Economy

This section summarizes the main points of several econometric studies I have performed using Chinese official data. Since the studies confirm well-established economic hypotheses using these data, the quality of the data and the validity of the hypotheses reinforce each other. However, we do not provide a systematic analysis of what kinds of errors can be tolerated in each study because that would make the paper too lengthy.

3.1 Descriptive statistics of the Chinese economy

In the process of writing Chow (1985), I used the *China Statistical Yearbook* to describe some facts about the Chinese economy. In the early 1980s, Western observers often claimed that Chinese official statistics were used to fool the outside world about China. This claim was supported by stories written by news reporters who had visited China and wrote glorifying stories during the period of the Cultural Revolution which were later found to be untrue. The fact that Chinese officials misled visitors about China has been well-documented. However, and somewhat surprisingly, such falsification did not survive when the *China Statistical Yearbook* began to be published in 1981.

Let me cite some examples. During the Great Leap Forward movement of 1958–61, Chairman Mao Zedong urged the farmers to increase their output at an unreasonable rate. Some communes did report much larger outputs than actually obtained and some such reports appeared in Chinese newspapers at the time. However, the value of gross agricultural output in constant 1957 prices reported in *China Statistical Yearbook 1981*, p. 17, was reduced from 53.7 billion yuan in 1957, the year before the Great Leap, to 43.0 billion in 1962, the year after the Great Leap, while national income in constant prices decreased by 31 percent from 1960 to 1961 (*Yearbook 1984*, p. 30).

Statistics on population was improved when China received help from the United Nations in the collection of population data in the early 1980s. Official statistics have been used by the Office of Population Research at Princeton University for demographic studies of the Chinese economy. According to *China Statistical Yearbook 1990*, p. 90, the death rates in 1958–62 were respectively 11.98, 14.59, 25.43, 14.24 and 10.02 per thousand persons while the birth rates in these years were respectively 29.22, 24.78, 20.86, 18.02 and 37.01. These data show the large increases in the death rate and substantial reductions in birth rate following the economic disaster created by the Great Leap Forward. Both suggest the starvation or malnutrition of the population during this period which the Chinese government did not attempt to conceal.

During the Cultural Revolution in 1966–76, when some Western reporters, having visited China, described the country as a utopia, *China Statistical*

Yearbook 1981, p. 451 reported that student enrollment in higher education was 48,000 in 1970 as compared with 750,000 in 1963 and 1,020,000 in 1979. The Cultural Revolution caused almost all universities to close, as the data reveal. Concerning the real wage of all state-owned units, *Yearbook 1981*, pp. 411–2 and 435–6, summarized in Chow (1985b, p. 143), gives the average annual wage per worker to be 637 yuan in 1957, the last normal year before the Great Leap, and 602 in 1977, the year before economic reform started. The reduction in real wage per worker is more since the general retail price index was 121.3 in 1957 and 135.0 in 1977. This reveals that during the 20 years of central planning from 1957 (the last year of the First Five-Year Plan) upto 1977, the real wage of the Chinese workers actually declined by 15 percent.

3.2 An aggregate model of national income determination

In Chow (1985) I used official data from 1953 to 1982 on national income, consumption and accumulation (investment) to estimate a simple model of the Chinese macroeconomy. I found the consumption function to satisfy the permanent income hypothesis of Hall (1978), which states that consumption is approximately a random walk, i.e., annual change in consumption cannot be predicted by past data, and the investment equation to satisfy the acceleration principle, i.e., investment is a function of the rate of change of income rather than the level of income. The permanent income hypothesis states that consumption is based on income in a longer time horizon than just the current year. The acceleration principle is based on the hypothesis that demand for capital stock depends on the level of output; since investment is the rate of change of capital stock, it will depend on the rate of change of income or output. These laws should apply to China as do many other economic laws used to study the Chinese economy summarized in Chow (2002). Deviations of observed values of national income from predictions based on this model revealed special historical-political events. The confirmation of two important hypotheses in macroeconomics using Chinese data provides supporting evidence for both the hypothesis and the reliability of the data.

3.3 Family expenditure patterns from cross-section data

The *China Statistical Yearbook* provides data on total consumption expenditures, and expenditures on food, clothing, housing and miscellaneous items for rural and urban populations. Using data for rural families in 1981, Chow (1985b) estimates linear relations between log expenditures on the above four categories and log total expenditures. The estimated total expenditure elasticities for China are similar to the estimates for other developing economies and the differences can be reasonably attributed to cultural and environmental factors. Furthermore, data for 1998 yield similar estimates as the above estimates based on 1981 data, as reported in Chow (2002, p. 161). The stability of the parameters estimated in the two years lends support to both the stability of Chinese consumer behavior over such a long period of time and the reliability of the data used.

3.4 An aggregate production function for China

Chow (1993) uses official data to construct a capital stock series of China. Together with annual data from 1952 to 1983 on national output and labor force, this series was used to estimate a Cobb–Douglas production function for total output and for the output of each of five sectors, agriculture, industry, construction, transport and trade. All parameter estimates are reasonable. Certain properties of the estimated production function for total output seem to make good economic sense. First, after accepting the hypothesis that the exponents of capital and labor sum to unity, it is found that the coefficients are approximately 0.6 and 0.4 respectively. This result agrees with Mankiw, Romer and Weil (1992) who estimated aggregate production functions for a number of developing economies. Furthermore, the capital exponent of

0.6 agrees with the result of a regression of log(output/labor) on log(capital/labor) using official data for state-owned industrial enterprises, as shown in Chow (1985, p. 123). Second, the intercept term measuring total factor productivity has no increasing trend up to 1979 and begins to increase at about 2.8 percent per year after reform started in 1979. This point is later elaborated in Chow (2002, Chapter 5) when a longer time series based on official data was available to estimate the production function.

3.5 Explaining inflation by the ratio of money supply to total output

Chow (1987) succeeded in explaining the rate of inflation in China from 1954 to 1983 using an error-correction model. The error correction model determines the rate of change in the price level by its past change and the change in the ratio of money supply to output, together with an error-correction term. The error-correction term is the deviation in the preceding period of log price level from its equilibrium level determined by the log of the ratio of money supply to real output. This equilibrium relation is called a cointegration relation and can be consistently estimated by a least-squares regression of log price on log(money supply/output). Note that during most of the years of the sample period, China was practicing central planning and yet the retail price index was affected by the ratio of money supply to output. The official index of retail prices shows a 16.2 percent inflation in 1961 which can be easily explained by the substantial increase in money supply and especially the very large reduction in real output from 1215.6 in 1960 to 838.7 in 1961 (see Table 1 of Chow, 1987). Economic theory and accuracy of official data again reinforce each other in this case.

3.6 Effects of monetary shocks on output and prices

As an extension of the study reported in Section 3.5, Chow and Shen (2004) use a VAR in the logs of money supply, price level and output to explain inflation and to study the responses of prices and output to monetary shocks. The result from the estimated impulse responses to monetary shocks agrees with the proposition of Milton Friedman (1994) that the response of output to money shocks takes place earlier but the effect is short-lived while the response of prices occurs later but lasts longer. This study is capable of explaining the increase in output in 2003 and 2004 and the increase in prices in 2004 in China following a rapid increase in money supply in 2002 after several years of a fairly slow and steady increase in money supply up to 2002 and the absence of inflation during these years. The increase in money supply can be attributed to the failure of the Chinese government to raise the exchange rate of the RMB. An undervalued RMB led to a large export surplus and a large inflow of foreign reserves (to an accumulated amount of over 600 billion dollars by the end of 2004). The increase in money supply is a result of people using foreign currency to exchange for RMB, and not of the policy of the People's Bank. The Chinese government tried to slow down this "overheated" economy by administrative means such as restricting the amount of credit to be extended by banks and new construction projects. Extensive credit extension to finance construction in urban development would not have occurred if the banks had not had the money to lend in the first place.

3.7 Estimating the economic loss of the Great Leap Forward and the Cultural Revolution

By constructing an econometric model consisting of an aggregate production, an identity for aggregate output as the sum of consumption and investment, an equation for capital stock as the sum of capital stock in the previous year plus net investment, and an equation specifying the logarithm of total factor productivity as a random walk with shift, Chow and Kwan (1996) and Kwan and Chow (1996) use a dynamic optimization model to explain per capita output, consumption and investment under the assumption that optimal investment was generated by an economic planner maximizing an infinitely discounted sum of future log per capita consumption. The model estimated by official data can explain the endogenous variables reasonably well. The time paths generated by eliminating the shocks for the "abnormal" years of the Great Leap Forward and the Cultural Revolution as a counterfactual experiment provide sensible estimates of the loss in terms of the endogenous variables due to these two tragic political events.

3.8 Demand for education

The study of demand for education in China by Chow and Shen (2005) was partly motivated by the striking fact that the ratio of total spending on education to GDP increased from 3.5 in 1998 to 5.2 in 2002. Was such a rapid increase due to a change in government policy or to basic economic forces of demand? The paper estimates demand functions for education at the three levels of primary school, secondary school and higher education and for total enrollment at all three levels. The income elasticities as estimated by cross-provincial data appear reasonable, with 0.4 for primary schools, 0.8 for secondary schools and 1.2 for higher education. Time series data from 1991 to 2002 were used to estimate price elasticities which turned out to be about 0.3 for all levels. Demand for total enrollment is divided into demand by non-government and government sources. The former depends on GDP and relative price while the latter depends on government revenue and relative price. Reasonable estimates of the elasticities were obtained. The demand equations from these two components can explain the rapid increase in the ratio of education spending to GDP very well. The fact that government revenue from 1998 to 2002 increased more rapidly than GDP helps to explain the rapid increase in the ratio of government spending on education to GDP. The small price elasticity of demand can explain the increase in total education spending in the course of economic development. As increase in income shifts the demand curve for education (student enrollment) upward against an inelastic supply, the relative price of education goes up. With a small price elasticity, the increase in price leads to an increase in total spending. Given a demand function for log enrollment Q as a linear function of log income Y and log price P with income and price elasticity denoted by a and $-b$ respectively, the demand for log (education expenditure) or log (PQ) is the same function with the coefficient of log P changed to $1 - b$. The log of (PQ/Y) equals a constant + $(a - 1)$ log Y + $(1 - b)$ log P. If income elasticity a is close to 1 or larger, an increase in income Y will have a small or a positive effect while the resulting increase in P due to limited supply of education services will have a positive effect on the ratio of education spending to national income. All parameters of this model are estimated using official data.

3.9 Explanation of the rate of return to schooling

Johnson and Chow (1997) estimate equations to explain log wage of Chinese rural and urban workers in 1988 by log S (years of schooling), years of experience E, E squared, and dummy variables representing gender, minority group and Communist Party membership following the classic work of Mincer (1974). The rate of return was estimated to be 4.02 percent per additional year of schooling and 3.39 percent for urban workers. Such low rates of return are reasonable because wages at the time were still substantially controlled and were not determined by market forces. The estimated effects of being a female (–0.085), an ethnic minority (–0.06 but not significant statistically) and a Communist Party member (+0.063) appear reasonable.

4 Examples of Errors in Official Data

In this section I provide examples of inaccurate official statistics, some discovered while doing econometric analysis of the Chinese economy.

First, on the number of persons in the labor force, *China Statistical Yearbook 1997* (Table 4–2, p. 94) gives the number of employed persons (in 10,000 persons) as 54,334 in 1988, 55,329 in 1989, 63,909 in 1990 and 64,799 in

1991. The increase from 1989 to 1990 is obviously too large to be believable. If we examine the employment data in *China Statistical Yearbook 1994* (p. 86), we find 55,329 for 1989, 56,740 for 1990 and 58,360 for 1991, with no obvious break in the data. Since the State Statistics Bureau made a major revision in the collection of data, the jump in the revised data (especially in the component for primary industry) may occur because of the difference in coverage or method of collection, but no explanation of the jump is given in the 1997 *Yearbook*. If the revised data are correct, then the data for 1989 and before must be erroneous.

As a second example, Chow and Shen (2005), in examining the data on non-government expenditures for education, point out that underestimation has resulted from the failure to include contributions from overseas Chinese, especially those living in Hong Kong. This conclusion is based on the first author's knowledge of specific large items that are excluded. The underestimation is due to the lack of coverage by the reporting units in the Department of Education which provides the data in the *Yearbook*. The Department of Education does not require educational institutions to report contributions from overseas Chinese as non-government expenditures on education. Substantial amounts from overseas Chinese contributed towards the construction of school buildings, many named after the donor, and visiting faculty members at universities and teachers in lower level educational institutions are not reported as part of non-government expenditures on education. In defense of the official data, it may be said that non-government education spending as provided by the Chinese National Bureau of Statistics covers only spending by Chinese nationals or institutions, and excludes spending by overseas Chinese. Under this interpretation there is no error; only the definition of spending is more restricted.

The third is concerned with statistical discrepancies in data on consumption. Statistical discrepancies almost always exist when two different sources are employed to measure the same phenomenon. A standard case is in the measurement of national income from final expenditures and from payments to factors of production. Final expenditures consist of consumption, investment, government expenditures and exports minus imports. Payments to factors include wages, rents, profits and interests. The two methods yield different results, creating a statistical discrepancy. A statistical discrepancy can be found when consumption is constructed for China's national income account which is partly based on retail sales data as compared with surveys of urban and rural households. Per capita consumption based on the national income account (NIA) can be much larger than that based on sample surveys, both reported in the *Statistical Yearbook*. For example, using *China Statistical Yearbook 1997* on data for 1996, NIA gives consumption of residence (excluding government consumption) as 32,589 (10,000 yuan) on p. 25, and population as 1,22,389 (10,000 persons) on p. 69, yielding per capita consumption of 2663 yuan per person. The survey data give urban consumption per capita as 3919.5 yuan on p. 294 and rural consumption per capita as 1572.1 yuan on p. 316. Since the fractions of urban and rural population in 1996 are respectively 0.2937 and 0.7063 (on p. 69), per capita consumption as a weighted mean is 2262, which is only 84.94 percent of the above NIA estimate. I owe this discovery to Holz (2004) who points out that the value of commodity consumption from NIA exceeds those based the surveys substantially for many years, as given in his Table 4.

Consumption reported in the national income account is larger than consumption obtained from sample surveys partly because it has a broader coverage. It includes consumption of goods and services provided by the units in which the consumers work and are not paid for by the consumers themselves (such as payment in kind and possibly medical expenses and schooling for the children), home production by the consumers, implicit rent of their housing units, and all other goods and services not paid for. Consumption as reported in sample surveys includes only goods and services paid for by the households themselves. Allowing for such differences in coverage, one may still find it difficult to explain the difference by a factor of 0.85 as given above. Holz (2004) has to reconcile the differences between the two sets of data but cannot explain the large differences.

5 Official Estimate of the Rate of GDP Growth

A number of studies have been published which are critical of particular data published in the *China Statistical Yearbook*. See for example the ten papers on different aspects of Chinese economic statistics published in *China Economic Review* 12, no. 4 (2001), edited by T. G. Rawski and W. Xiao. There are also the opposite viewpoints of Maddison (1998) and Holz (2004b) concerning the possible overestimation of economic growth by Chinese official statistics. It is not the purpose of this paper to review the points of each of these articles and other related articles in the literature. I will confine my discussion to certain diverse opinions on the rate of growth of real output in China.

The rate of growth of GDP as estimated by official data is discussed by Rawski (2001) and Klein and Ozmucur (2002/2003). The former is critical and the latter is supportive of the official estimate. Rawski (2001, Table 1) cites data on energy use, urban formal employment and consumer price index which grew much more slowly than the rate of growth of GDP in the years 1998–2001 to argue for the overestimation of GDP in official data. Holz (2003) raises doubts about the above argument for data inaccuracy.

Klein and Ozmucur (2002/2003) use a more comprehensive set of 15 related time series and regress the rate of growth of GDP on four principal components (linear combinations that are mutually uncorrelated) extracted from the rates of change of these 15 series, and find the relation to be close and the regression coefficients to be reasonable. The 15 series are electricity (kwh), coal (tons), oil (tons), steel (tons), freight (ton*km), civil aviation (ton*km), long-distance telephone calls, employment share of tertiary sector, gain output, exports (const. $), imports (const. $), government spending (deflated), real wage, inflation rate (cpi) and livestock products (tons). The sample period is from 1980 to 2000. Klein and Ozmucur appear to be more convincing than Rawski because the related series used are more comprehensive and the sample period is longer.

Rawski (2001) cites casual evidence from statements of Chinese economists and even Premier Zhu Rongji about possible data falsification due to political pressure, but also points out that the National Statistics Bureau has tried to correct the possible over- or under-reporting of Chinese output data. It is interesting to observe that the official growth rates for 2002, 2003 and 2004 remain as high as 8.0, 9.6 and 9.3 respectively while the Chinese government openly claimed that the economy was overheating in 2003 and 2004 and tried to use macro-control policies to slow it down. If the National Statistics Bureau follows political winds, how could its estimates for GDP growth be as high as reported in 2003 and 2004? If the rate of growth of real GDP in 1999–2001 had been as low as Rawski (2001) suggests, how could economic growth increase suddenly to such high rates in the following few years? If the official growth rates of 2002–2004 are also overestimates, how can such overestimates of growth be maintained for a six-year period without making the estimate in 2004 look very unreasonable, given the initial estimate of real GDP in 1998?

Young (2003) also claims that the official estimate of the annual rate of growth of real GDP and of industrial output from 1978 to 1998 was about two percentage points too high. I have pointed out why Young was incorrect in Chapter 20. Chow (2004) attempted to reproduce the estimates of real GDP for 1988 and 1989 by the method of Young and to pinpoint where they might lead to inaccurate results. Table 2 summarizes the data and the reproduction.

Table 2. Outputs and their rates of change in 1988 and 1989 by Young's method.

	GDP	Primary	Secondary	Construction	Tertiary
1988					
Nominal value	14928.3	3831.0	6587.2	810.0	4510.1
1989					
Nominal value	16909.2	4228.0	7278.0	794.0	5403.2
Price index (1988 = 1.0)		1.1501	1.186	1.186	1.239
Output in 1988 prices	14173.7	3676.2	6136.6	669.5	4360.9
Output change, 1988 = 1	0.94945	0.95959	0.93159	0.82654	0.96692

Notes: Data on nominal outputs are found in *CSY 1997* (Table 2-9). Price index for primary industry is purchasing price index for farm products (1978 = 100) given in *CSY 1997* (Table 8-11) converted to (1988 = 1.0). Price index for secondary industry is ex-factory price index of industrial products given in *CSY 1997* (Table 8-12). Price index for tertiary industry is the price index of the service component of the consumer price index (*CSY 1990*, Table 7-17). 1989 output in 1988 prices for each of the three components of GDP is obtained by deflating nominal output by the corresponding price index. GDP in 1988 prices is the sum of the above three components.

The resulting 5.15 percent decline in real GDP is made up of a decline of 4.14 percent in the primary industry, 6.84 percent in the secondary industry and 3.31 percent in the tertiary industry. I have pointed out in the last paragraph that a negative growth of 6.84 percent for the secondary industry is a very unreasonable estimate. Furthermore, if we deflate the nominal value of construction 794.0 in 1989 by the ex-factory industrial price index of 1.186 (1988 = 1.0) to obtain its value of 669.5 in 1988 prices, we obtain a rate of change of 1 − 0.8265 = −0.1735 for construction as given by Young's method. This alleged negative 17 percent rate of decline in construction is highly inconsistent with the reported rate of increase in completed floor space by 3.5 percent. The calculation for the growth rate in 1989 pinpoints one specific large error resulting from Young's method. Therefore the method of Young (2003) for estimating the rate of change of real output can be very unreliable. In fact the large discrepancy between Young's estimate of negative

5.2 percent and the official estimate of positive 4 percent for the year 1989 alone contributes to almost half a percentage point in the difference between the two estimates of the average annual growth rate for the entire sample period of 1978–1998.

6 Conclusion

Although Chinese official data have been widely used for economic research published in refereed journals, there are still critics who claim that the data may be falsified for political purposes. This paper points out that staff members of the Chinese National Statistical Bureau in Beijing and in its provincial and city offices are obligated by law to provide accurate statistics, that the statistics are used for national economic planning as reported by the Premier to the National People's Congress and read by observers all over the world, that it is difficult to falsify national output and other statistics for a long period and that even in selected years between 1996 and 2005 official annual GDP growth rates appear reasonable. It reaches the conclusion that the official data are by and large reliable, granted unavoidable errors in certain cases, by drawing on the author's own experience in using them for many economic studies where data accuracy and the confirmation of well-established economic hypotheses reinforced each other. It examines the arguments of certain critics of official estimates of output growth rates and exposes the errors in the alternative estimates. Needless to say, any serious scholar using the Chinese official data, as in using any other data, would need to exercise caution in his research even if the data are not purposely falsified.

Acknowledgments

The author would like to thank Carsten Holz and three anonymous referees for valuable comments on an earlier draft of this paper and the Gregory C.

Chow Econometric Research Program of Princeton University for research support.

References

Chow, Gregory C. "A model of national income determination in China." *Journal of Political Economy*, 93 (1981): 782–792.

Chow, Gregory C. *The Chinese Economy*. New York: Harper and Row, 1985.

Chow, Gregory C. "Chinese statistics." *The American Statistician*, 40 (1986): 191–196.

Chow, Gregory C. "Money and price determination in China." *Journal of Comparative Economics*, 11 (1987): 319–333.

Chow, Gregory C. "Capital formation and economic growth in China." *Quarterly Journal of Economics*, 108 (1993): 809–842.

Chow, Gregory C. *China's Economic Transformation*. Oxford: Blackwell Publishing, 2002.

Chow, Gregory C. *Knowing China*. Singapore: World Scientific Publishing Co., 2004.

Chow, Gregory C. and Kwan, Y. K. "Economic effects of political movements in China: Lower bound estimates." *Pacific Economic Review*, 1 (1996): 13–26.

Chow, Gregory C. and Shen, Yan. "Money, price level and output in the Chinese macro-economy." Princeton University, Center for Economic Policy Studies, 2004.

Chow, Gregory C. and Shen, Yan. "Demand for education in China." Princeton University, mimeo, 2005.

Friedman, Milton. *Money Mischiefs*. New York: Harcourt Brace & Company, 1994.

Hall, Robert E. "Stochastic implications of the life cycle-permanent income hypothesis: Theory and statistical evidence." *Journal of Political Economy*, 86 (December 1978): 971–987.

Holz, Carsten A. "Fast, clear and accurate: how reliable are Chinese output and economic growth statistics." *China Quarterly* 173, (2003): 122–163.

Holz, Carsten A. "Deconstructing China's GDP statistics." *China Economic Review* 15, no. 2 (2004a): 164–202.

Holz, Carsten A. "China's reform period economic growth: Why Angus Maddison got it wrong and what that means." Hong Kong University of Science and Technology, Department of Social Science working paper, December 2004b.

Holz, Carsten A. "OECD – China Governance Project: The Institutional Arrangements for the Production of Statistics." *OECD Statistics Working Papers*, 2005/1, OECD Publishing, 2005.

Johnson, Emily N. and Chow, Gregory. "Rates of return to schooling in China." *Pacific Economic Review* 2, no. 2 (1997): 101–113.

Klein, Lawrence R. and Ozmucur S. "The estimation of China's economic growth rate." *Journal of Economic and Social Measurement*, 28 (2002/2003): 187–202.

Kwan, Y. K. and Chow, Gregory C. "Estimating economic effects of political movements in China." *Journal of Comparative Economics*, 23 (1996): 192–208.

Maddison, Angus. *Chinese Economic Performance in the Long Run*. Paris: Development Centre of the Organization of Economic Co-operation and Development, 1998.

Mankiw, N. Gregory, David Romer and Cavid N. Weil. "A contribution to the empirics of economic growth." *Quarterly Journal of Economics*, 107 (1992): 407–438.

Mincer, Jacob. *Schooling, Experience and Earnings*. New York: Columbia University Press, 1974.

People's Republic of China. State Statistical Bureau. *China Statistical Yearbook*. Beijing: China Statis. Pub. House, annual issues.

People's Republic of China. State Statistical Bureau. *China Commodity Prices Statistical Yearbook* (in Chinese, Zhongguo Wujia Tongji Nianjian). Beijing: China Statis. Pub. House, annual issues.

Rawski, T. G. "What is happening to China's GDP statistics?" *China Economic Review* 12, no. 4 (2001): 347–354.

Rawski, T. G. and W. Xiao (guest editors). "Roundtable on Chinese economic statistics: Introduction." *China Economic Review* 12, no. 4 (2001): 298–302.

Republic of China. *Statistical Yearbook of the Republic of China*. Taipei: Directorate-General of Budget, Accounting and Statistics, annual issucs.

Young, Alwyn, "Gold into base metals: Productivity growth in the People's Republic of China during the reform period." *Journal of Political Economy*, 111 (2003): 1220–1261.

22

Will China Experience Serious Inflation?

There has been much concern about inflation in China recently. The People's Bank in the last few months has raised the reserve requirement several times to control the money supply to slow down inflation. In 1985 when I was organizing a summer workshop on macroeconomics in cooperation with the Ministry of Education, Premier Zhao Ziyang asked me to forecast inflation for 1985–1986 because in 1984 the supply of money in the form of currency in circulation increased by 50 percent. I estimated an equation using data from 1952 to 1984 to explain inflation and used the equation to project forward to forecast an inflation rate for 1985 of no more than 9 percent which turned out to be correct. This equation was published in Chow (1987, Eq. 18) and was updated using data up to 2004 in Chow (2007, pp. 34–5). The data are given in Table 1.

Most recently I have updated this equation using data from 1952 to 2009 and found that the same equation fits the data for the entire period. Furthermore I have divided the data into two periods, data up to 1978 when economic reform started and data after 1979. I apply The Chow test to find out whether the coefficients of the regression equation changed in the two periods and found that the data strongly support the assumption that there was no change in these coefficients. Readers may be surprised by this result because in the first period China had a planned economy. The fact is that even in this period, inflation followed the same economic law.

This equation is based on the quantity theory of money $Mv = PY$, where M is money supply, P is a price index and Y is real output. PY is GDP in money terms and Y is GDP in real terms. Based on this equation, the most important variable to explain P is M/Y. Note that in 1961 there was over 16 percent inflation according to Chinese official data mainly because of the big reduction in Y by 30 percent, as a result of the economic collapse of the Great Leap Forward which began in 1958. I have plotted the data of log P against $\log(M/Y)$ for the entire period from 1952 to 2009 and found they fall fairly close to a straight line. This shows that the most important variable to explain log P is indeed $\log(M/Y)$. Furthermore, the deviations of the values of P from the above straight line show when inflation is above or below normal. If the deviation is positive or the actual value of log P is above the line, P in that year is above normal and there is a tendency for P to return to normal in the following year.

Inflation is the rate of change in P, or the change in log P. It is explained by three variables: the rate of change in (M/Y), inflation of the last year because of inertia, and the deviation in the previous year of log P from the line as explained in the last paragraph. The coefficients of the three variables are respectively 0.149, 0.525 and –0.156 if data from 1952 to 2009 are used to estimate the equation. Here, P is the retail price index and M is $M2$. The average error of this equation in explaining past inflation is 3.4 percent.

In more technical terms, the model used to forecast inflation in 2010 is an error correction model (ECM) estimated as follows:

In the first stage, I have estimated

$$\log(P_t) = -0.698\ (0.0277) + 0.367\ (0.0080)\ \log(M2_t/Y_t) + u_t$$

R-square = 0.974; S.E. of regression = 0.095.

The number in parentheses after each coefficient is its standard error.

The result is plotted in Fig. 1 below.

Let $u_t = \log(P_t) - \log(P_t^*)$ be the estimated deviation of the log P from the above equation. I then regress $\Delta\log(P_t)$ on $\text{dlog}(M2_t/Y_t)$, $\text{dlog}(P_{t-1})$, and u_{t-1} where $\text{dlog}(X_t)$ is defined as $\log(X_t) - \log(X_{t-1})$, following the regression of Chow (1987).

$$\begin{aligned}\text{dlog}(P_t) = {} & 0.0002\ (0.0057) + 0.149\ (0.0407)\ \text{dlog}(M2_t/Y_t) \\ & + 0.525(0.0899)\ \text{dlog}(P_{t-1}) \\ & - 0.156\ (0.0485)\ u_{t-1}\end{aligned}$$

R-square = 0.624; S.E. of regression = 0.034

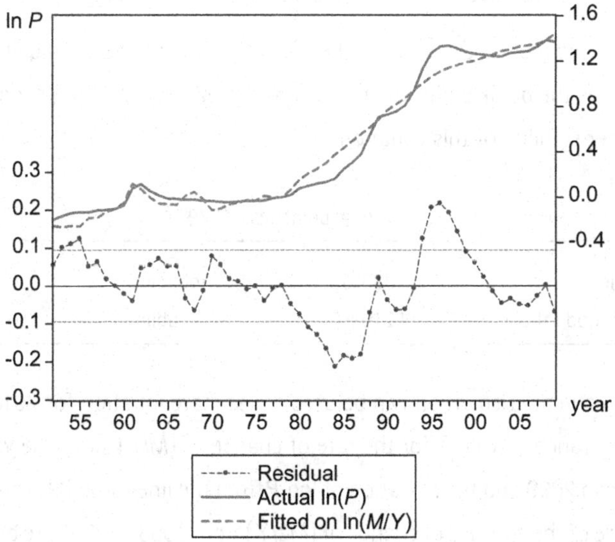

Fig. 1.

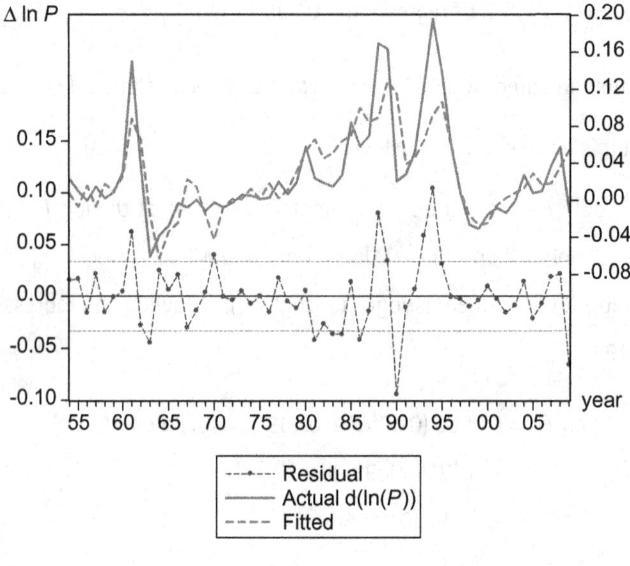

Fig. 2.

The data on inflation and its predicted value are shown in Fig. 2.

The following reports the result of the Chow test for parameter stability using $t = 1979$ as the break point. The result provides extremely strong support for parameter stability of this equation.

Chow Breakpoint Test: 1979

F-statistic	0.938525	Probability	0.449788
Log likelihood ratio	4.216950	Probability	0.377440

The last estimated equation can be used to estimate inflation for 2010 if we assume a range of values for the rate of change of (M/Y) since the value of inflation in 2009 and the deviation of log P from the line for 2009 are known. The range of the six rates of change of $(M2/Y)$ from 2003 to 2008 are between 3.27 percent and 8.68 percent and the rate of change in 2009 is 17.4 percent.

The following table gives the prediction of inflation for different reasonable values of the rate of change of ($M2/Y$).

$\Delta\log(M2/GDP)$	3.00%	6.00%	9.00%	12.00%	15.00%	18.00%
$\Delta\log(P)$	0.91%	1.35%	1.80%	2.25%	2.69%	3.14%

Since the rate of increase in ($M2/Y$) in 2009 was an outlier, it is reasonable to predict from the above table that the rate of inflation itself would range from 0.91percent to 2.69 percent as measured by the increase in the general retail price index. The rate of inflation for 2010 will be moderate mainly because of

Table 1. Price level and its determinants (1952–2009).

Year	Index of retail price (P)	$M2$	Real GDP index (Y)
1952	0.8227	74.50314	22
1953	0.8506	82.00875	25.1
1954	0.8705	90.20963	26.6
1955	0.8793	94.85521	28.3
1956	0.8793	132.3043	32.3
1957	0.8926	139.0515	33.7
1958	0.8947	194.0242	41.2
1959	0.9028	226.401	44.6
1960	0.9308	256.6131	43.9
1961	1.082	286.1142	30.9
1962	1.1229	233.48	28.9
1963	1.0567	214.0444	32
1964	1.0177	214.5185	37.2
1965	0.9904	246.5319	43.5
1966	0.9875	285.2925	50.9
1967	0.9801	309.5001	44.5

(Continued)

Table 1. (*Continued*).

Year	Index of retail price (*P*)	*M*2	Real GDP index (*Y*)
1968	0.9809	335.6512	44.2
1969	0.9698	336.8679	52.7
1970	0.9676	320.8612	65
1971	0.9603	357.9469	69.5
1972	0.9581	404.8609	71.5
1973	0.9639	454.3348	77.5
1974	0.9691	494.3595	78.3
1975	0.9706	525.0772	84.9
1976	0.9735	573.4608	82.6
1977	0.9934	595.6617	89
1978	1	668.1896	100
1979	1.02	867.0332	107.6
1980	1.081	1178.303	116
1981	1.107	1453.783	122.1
1982	1.128	1761.087	133.1
1983	1.145	2247.387	147.6
1984	1.177	3171.021	170
1985	1.281	4188.024	192.9
1986	1.358	5460.866	210
1987	1.457	7154.482	234.3
1988	1.727	9378.91	260.7
1989	2.034	11836.63	271.3
1990	2.077	15293.4	281.7
1991	2.137	19349.9	307.6
1992	2.252	25402.2	351.4
1993	2.549	34879.8	400.4
1994	3.102	46923.5	452.8
1995	3.561	60750.5	502.3
1996	3.778	76094.9	552.6
1997	3.808	90995.3	603.9

(*Continued*)

Table 1. (*Continued*).

Year	Index of retail price (*P*)	*M2*	Real GDP index (*Y*)
1998	3.709	104498.5	651.2
1999	3.598	119897.9	700.9
2000	3.544	134610.3	759.9
2001	3.516	158301.9	823
2002	3.47	185007	897.8
2003	3.467	221222.8	987.8
2004	3.564	254107	1087.4
2005	3.593	298755.7	1200.8
2006	3.629	345603.6	1340.7
2007	3.767	403442.2	1515.5
2008	3.989	475166.6	1651.2
2009	3.940	606224	1794.9

the inertia imbedded in the inflation process as given by our equation to explain inflation. This is the same reason why inflation in 1985 was no more than 9 percent when money supply increased by 50 percent in 1984. Before 1984, inflation rates in China were small. However, if M/Y is to keep increasing fairly rapidly for several years from now, more serious inflation will result, just as continued rapid increases in M during the years of 1985 to 1988 caused serious inflation in 1989. The People's Bank is correct in tightening the supply of money now. The effort to restrict the increase of M/Y needs to be continued to maintain price stability in China.

Acknowledgments

I would like to acknowledge the help of Niu Linlin of Xiamen University in the preparation of this paper.

References

Chow, Gregory C. "Money and price level determination in China." *Journal of Comparative Economics*, 11 (1987): 319–333.

Chow, Gregory C. *China's Economic Transformation*, 2nd ed. Malden, MA: Blackwell Publishers, 2007.

State Statistics Bureau of the People's Republic of China. *China Statistical Yearbook* 2009.

23

How to Put "Seek Truth from Facts" into Practice

The success of China's economic reform and economic development has been due to a large extent to the practice of "seek truth from facts" to find out what the appropriate reform policies should be. Let me examine how this principle can be further applied, not only by the Party and the government, but also by the Chinese people, in order to promote even more rapid progress of the Chinese economy and society.

In seeking truth, we need an attitude of objectivity, recognizing that one's own opinion can be wrong and respecting the opinions of others which may be different from our own.

Many university students in China do not raise questions to their teachers sufficiently because they believe that by doing so they would undermine the latter's authority. This attitude is mistaken. Surely students should respect their teachers, but in discussing intellectual topics they should freely express their opinions while still respecting their teachers. The teachers would lose out in seeking truth from facts if they do not allow students to express their opinions freely because some opposing opinions will lead them to understand the subject better.

I once wrote an article on China's population problem and policy. The article was hotly debated on the internet. As of 8:55am, June 6, 2009, one particular website recorded 494 persons having expressed agreement and 161 persons having expressed disagreement.

Among the latter, some said, "All this is rubbish...", "Such a foolish scholar, making statements that are of no scientific value..." There are other equally insulting remarks. I was somewhat surprised by the language that some of my readers use and the lack of respect they have for opinions that are different from theirs.

On the topic of friendly and respectful exchanges of opposing opinions, I recall a set of emails between Professor Ronald McKinnon and me on whether the exchange rate of the Chinese RMB should be revalued. The exchanges were published in *International Economic Review* 11–12, 2005. The editor introducing the exchange writes, "The editor expresses admiration for the attitude of these scholarly exchanges that are perhaps difficult to find in the exchanges among the present-day Chinese scholars." When I read the editor's remarks I began to realize that exchanges of opposite views among Chinese scholars may not be friendly and respectful.

Possibly, if the above behavior is true, it has to do with China's cultural tradition cultivated under the rule of an emperor. The subjects should obey the emperor and should not say anything against his rule, including all his statements. Today, however, we are in the process of modernization. We are seeking truth from facts. For this purpose, discussion and polite debate are essential. As I have pointed out, the reason to be polite and respectful of those with opposing views from ours is not just courtesy but the need to cultivate a spirit of objectivity in inquiry. We should think objectively客观地思考, allowing for the possibility that we are wrong. If we tolerate our own mistakes we will begin to learn also to tolerate other people's mistakes. Reaching the right conclusions in science and in action depends on this attitude. Once we have cultivated this attitude, we can begin to learn and to make better policies.

In order to change such bad habits in China, I believe that the following rules are useful:

Rule 1. Do not criticize or attack the person, but only criticize his ideas that are different from ours. This rule was violated by the critics of my article on the population problem of China quoted above.

Rule 2. We need to cultivate an attitude of humility, allowing for the possibility that our ideas are wrong.

Rule 3. If we discover we are wrong, frankly and openly admit our mistakes.

Rule 4. If you discover others are wrong, continue to respect them. They will also respect you in the future when you are wrong. Respect is mutual.

Schools in China differ from the schools in the US by teaching ethics and good behavior to students. In American universities, the students study academic subjects and have plenty of opportunities to develop social skills, participate in sports and engage in other extracurricula activities like playing musical instruments, but do not learn how to be a better citizen from the teachers. Students can participate in religious activities sponsored by different religious organizations which may be active in a university. I understand that in Chinese universities, good behavior and ethics are taught. I believe that the attitude to "seek truth from facts" discussed in this article should be part of the teaching in Chinese schools. Young students should begin expressing their ideas and learn to debate politely with others in class, including the teachers. By teaching this attitude and habit, the teachers themselves, who may have the bad habits in the first place, will learn and develop a better habit and attitude while teaching the students to do so. This is an example of "teaching is mutual growth," as an old Chinese saying goes.

Part 3

Economic Policy

24

From Economic Research to Social Change

A main theme of this article is that important steps after research are required before social changes can take place. Hence these steps should be anticipated while the research is being done. Much of the material of this chapter is drawn from my experience in applying the knowledge of economics to consult for a corporate vice president of IBM in the late 1960s, and to advise the government of Taiwan from the late 1960s to the early 1980s and top government officials of the People's Republic of China after the early 1980s.

From my experience I have learned that academic knowledge, even to the degree of being recognized by publications in top professional journals, is not sufficient for advising government officials on economic policy. This situation is perhaps similar to that of medical doctors engaged in successful research in medical science but having limited ability to treat patients. I have also learned some lessons on how to effect social changes based on my experience which I hope to share with readers.

1 A Gap Between Academic Knowledge and the Ability to Apply It to Solve Practical Problems

First-class academic economists have failed to see which parts of economics to apply in making suitable policy recommendations. They recognize this when they start serving as advisers in government positions, as many do by taking academic leave of absence to work in the government. For example, academic macroeconomic economists might not have the ability to advise the Federal Reserve on monetary policy without actual experience. Those who have spent time in Washington can testify that they have learned to provide policy advice through experience. The inability of macroeconomists in general to give policy advice is analogous to the inability of microeconomic theorists to serve as CEOs of major corporations.

Economics is a science for understanding economic phenomena, and can be used in both explaining and in predicting certain economic phenomena. This aspect of economics is known as positive economics. Normative economics deals with deciding what is good and what is bad. If economic analysis can point to one way of allocating given resources to yield a collection of outputs that can exceed the outputs allocated by another way, it can serve as a tool to improve the economy. Normative economics is used for such a purpose. From the nature of economic science as just described, one cannot guarantee that professional economists are necessarily capable of advising governments on economic policy. Having a solid training in economics, one understands how the economy works. However, while such an understanding is necessary, it is not a sufficient condition for giving good practical advice. Other qualifications are required.

What are these other qualifications? First, we need an ability to recognize which part of economic knowledge is relevant for application to the given practical economic problem at hand. A doctor who is trained in medical science may not always give the right treatment to a patient. This can come about when the doctor fails to recognize the nature of the illness that the patient has. Having the knowledge that a certain treatment is good for a certain illness does not imply knowing the illness a particular patient has.

Two examples illustrate this point. First, it has been suggested that economists at the International Monetary Fund failed to diagnose the problems of some economies during the East Asian financial crisis of 1997–9. When the problem was a lack of liquidity, the policy recommended was to introduce discipline to government spending, which was just the opposite of what the situation required. Second, when formulating policies for developing economies, one distinguished economist working in the US government suggested a significant increase in investment in human capital by increasing the number of primary and secondary schools. He failed to recognize that in many developing countries there are not enough qualified teachers to teach in the large number of primary and secondary schools needed under his policy.

I can use myself as an example in failing to recognize what economic tools were relevant for application to solve particular problems until others who were more experienced pointed them out to me. In 1966, when I took my first trip to Taiwan, I was an academic economist with solid publications in major journals and tenure or full professorship at Ivy League universities. I was fortunate to have the opportunity to serve as a junior member of a team of economists, led by the late T. C. Liu and S. C. Tsiang, who were considered chief advisers to the government of the Republic of China in Taiwan under the leadership of President Chiang Kai-shek. In 1967, President Chiang personally appointed us as his economic advisers. I began to realize that when a practical economic problem appeared, it was not easy to decide what economic tools, if any, should be applied. The same situation presents itself in pure economic research also. A research economist needs to decide what economic tools to apply to solve a given research problem. It was through practical experience in Taiwan that I first learned how to apply economic knowledge to solve real life problems.

2 A Gap Between Choosing the Right Economic Knowledge for Application and Making a Sound Policy Recommendation

Let us now assume that the economist recognizes which economic theory is relevant to the practical problem at hand. A good policy recommendation may not automatically follow. As I pointed out before, understanding is a necessary but not a sufficient condition for finding a good solution. Understanding why some part of an economy fails to work properly does not imply knowing how to fix it.

One example comes from my experience of serving as a consultant to, or perhaps an overseas member of, the State Commission for Reconstructing the Economic System, briefly called the Economic Reform Commission, of the People's Republic of China in the 1980s. The Commission was chaired by the Premier, Zhao Ziyang at the time, to show the importance of its work although the usual working meetings were chaired by Vice Chairman An Ziwen.

A major issue was the reform of the price system. In China, reform towards a market economy began in 1978. The first major success was the reform of the agricultural sector when collective farming under the commune system was changed to private farming, although the term "private farming" was not used officially. The new system was called the household responsibility system. Under this system each farm household was assigned a piece of land to farm and allowed to keep the products after paying a fixed amount which is equivalent to a fixed rent. By elementary economics we understand that paying a fixed charge does not interfere with deciding on the optimum amount of output by equating marginal cost and marginal revenue. Since farm production is essentially self-sufficient, prices of materials do not enter into optimum production calculations. The next step in China's economic reform was to improve the efficiency of state-owned enterprises, first by allowing them to make certain input and outcome decisions. Since state-owned enterprises needed to obtain materials for their production and needed to sell their outputs to obtain revenue, decontrol of prices was essential to ensure the efficient use of resources by the state enterprises. In the discussion of price reform, one major issue was to decide how to change the price of housing when the rent paid by the employees-tenants of state enterprises was set as low as four or five yuan per month.

In this example we knew the problem – that certain prices were set too low as judged by the conditions of market demand and supply. If prices are not determined by market forces, there cannot be efficient allocation of resources because low prices would lead to waste in the use of resources and high prices would prohibit the appropriate use of resources. This problem was clearly understood, but we needed to decide how to solve it.

The Economic Reform Commission was able to provide an excellent solution. It was to allow a two-tier price system. The two-tier price system was applied to the pricing in several important markets. In the case of residential housing, the existing tenants were given the right to stay in their apartments at low rents. Increasing the rent would cause social unrest because it is always difficult to take away entitlements that privileged groups have long enjoyed, just like the US government gave subsidies to farmers for years. In the meantime commercial housing was allowed to be built and sold or rented at higher market prices. Those who could afford to pay for commercial housing were welcome to enjoy it. This solution to the housing problem was a Pareto improvement since no one was worse off and some people became better off, living in better and more expensive commercial housing. A second example was the pricing of raw materials supplied to state enterprises. The government continued to supply such materials at low prices as before though in limited quantities, and allowed additional supply in the market to be sold at higher market prices. Since marginal calculations by the state enterprises were based on the higher market prices of the last units of inputs purchased, efficient production was achieved. Or to put this point differently, providing a fixed amount of subsidy to state enterprises in the form of charging them a low price for a fixed quantity of materials supplied to them would not affect their efficient calculations. Third, although foreign exchange was supplied at a fixed exchange rate (that overvalued the RMB just the opposite of the undervaluation of the RMB as of 2008), the quantity supplied was rationed. However, there was a swap center in Shanghai where importers and exporters could trade foreign exchange at a market rate which was higher for US dollars than the official rate but foreign exchange was made available. In sum, the two-tier price system enabled efficient allocation of resources during the transitional period of market reform in China.

The reader might think that the above policy was based on such a simple idea that any practicing economist could have thought of it. A good idea looks simple once someone points it out and applies it correctly in the right practical situation. By comparison, consider the experience of the former Soviet Union and some Eastern European economies which adopted a "shock treatment" to economic reform by decontrolling prices overnight and by privatizing a large number of state enterprises within some 500 days. This policy led to a collapse in industrial production when state-owned enterprises were sold hastily to opportunistic investors who did not intend to manage them but purchased them at very low prices for resale. In adopting shock treatment as the policy for economic reform, the governments of these countries were following the advice of some well-known American economists who understood the virtues of a market economy. This case illustrates that a knowledge of economics does not guarantee good sense in providing advice on economy policy.

3 Important Points to Note in Giving Economic Advice

In the last section I pointed out that having good sense or good judgment in providing economic advice is a talent not necessarily possessed by professional economists. In this section I would like to point out some important considerations in giving advice on economic policy, assuming that the economist involved has such good judgment.

First is the consideration of the feasibility of the policy. One should not give advice which is politically or otherwise not feasible to achieve. Economists with their set ideals are often emotionally involved and cannot refrain from preaching them to others even when the ideal recommendations have no chance of being adopted. Sometimes when they sell their ideas to responsible government officials, they may even lose the latter's confidence, making it more difficult to give their advice later even when it is achievable.

Second is the choice of the right government officials to work with. An economic adviser should have good judgment in finding the right government officials to work with. If a potential adviser knows that no important officials can understand or appreciate her viewpoint, she should not attempt to advise them. It may occur that good ideas go wasted because of the lack of appreciation by those with the power to adopt them, but we should accept this as a reality. To force good ideas on the wrong people would be counterproductive and would not lead to fruitful results. By the right government official, I mean one who can understand the virtue of your recommendation and also has enough leadership quality to adopt a good proposal as a government policy. I have met top government leaders who are not forceful enough to push good ideas through for adoption as government policy. Having the trust of such a leader is not of much use in affecting social change.

Third is the choice of timing even if a potential adviser has found government officials intelligent enough to appreciate her ideas. If she tries to push her ideas at the wrong moment, she will not find receptive ears and obtain a favorable reception.

Fourth, an adviser needs to be open-minded and to recognize the possibility that he might be wrong. My own experience in working with members of the Economic Reform Commission in China has taught me important lessons about economics in action. Many a time, fellow members of the Economic Reform Commission corrected my mistakes or taught me economics that I did not know. I have learned as much from them as they might have learned from me. That is why interactive discussions to search for appropriate economic policies is a good strategy to follow.

Let me elaborate on the interactive nature of my experience in advising both the Taiwan and the PRC governments. In Taiwan in the 1970s, there was a "Small Group of Five" consisting of the Governor of the Central Bank, the Minister of Economic Affairs, the Ministry of Finance, the Director General of Budget, Accounting and Statistics and the Secretary of the Executive Yuan. These were the government officials responsible for formulating and carrying out major economic policies in Taiwan at the time. When the group of overseas advisers reported to work in the summers, we sat around an oval-shaped table, with the five of them sitting opposite the five of us, to meet for one whole week in the mornings from nine to twelve. Each minister in turn would bring up his current economic problems for discussion while we listened, made comments and asked clarifying questions. After the first week, we went back to our offices to think and research possible solutions to the problems presented before us. This was a case when research was performed to solve specific practical economic problems. We met to exchange ideas and research results in small groups of two to three or as an entire team. After about six to eight weeks, the two groups met jointly. We presented our initial recommendations while the officials in the Small Group of Five made comments and raised questions before a final draft of our recommendations were written up. The final draft was published in newspapers and became an important document having substantial impact on economic policy.

Serious discussions also took place with the same, or perhaps even higher, intensity in meetings with members of the Economic Reform Commission of the PRC. We met each time for about four to five days from nine to five. I invited selected members of the Taiwan team, insofar as possible, to participate as well. Members of this team were economists favoring a market economy rather than a planned economy that the PRC had in the early 1980s. In the 1980s T. C. Liu had already passed away and S. C. Tsiang was still a top economic adviser to the government in Taiwan so it was not convenient for him to take part, but I succeeded in inviting him in March 1989 to meet with members of the Economic Reform Commission including An Ziwen, Vice Chairman of the Reform Commission, and Liu Hongru, Deputy Governor of China's Central Bank (and an enthusiastic reader of Milton Friedman's work), by arranging the meeting in Hong Kong.

The most pressing economic issue for China in March 1989 was the control of inflation. Our solution, the tried and proven solution of S. C. Tsiang to cure the inflation in Taiwan in the 1950s, was to raise the interest rate to ensure a positive real return to bank deposits. The Commission adopted our recommendation. We were confident that it would work and it did. (The economic analysis of inflation during this period is beyond the scope of our discussion here; interested readers may refer to Chow and Shen (2006).) In all meetings the discussions with members of the Economic Reform Commission were completely free and not restricted by ideological constraints of Communism. One economic official said to me once in the 1980s that China was willing to adopt any economic tools that were found useful in a capitalist economy. In sum, the open and interactive exchanges with economic officials in both Taiwan and mainland China have taught me a great deal about economics in

practice and the broad perspectives required to solve real-life economic problems.

4 Using the Framework of Dynamic Optimization to Provide Economic Policy Advice

The application of dynamic optimization to economics was the major area of my research from 1969 to 1979. While working at the IBM Thomas J. Watson Research Center in the late 1960s, my research interests shifted from econometric theory and econometric modeling to dynamic economics that includes the study of the dynamic properties of econometric models and the use of such models for macroeconomic policy analysis. In Chow (1970) I first applied the method of Lagrange multipliers to solve dynamic optimization problems in economics. In Chow (1975), both my Lagrange method and Bellman's method of dynamic programming were used to solve optimal control problems. At that time I thought seriously of using optimal control or the method of dynamic optimization in conjunction with a macroeconomic model to find an optimal control rule for the setting of macroeconomic policies.

Dynamic economics was a major area of my research. There was in the late 1970s a critique by Robert Lucas (1976) suggesting that the use of optimal control as a basis for economic policy advice was inappropriate because the parameters of the econometric model used would change as economic agents react to the control rule of the government. Although many economists were persuaded by Lucas, others including Chris Sims (1980), Ray Fair (1986) and myself believed that his critique might be valid in principle but has only limited relevance in practice because economic agents are not as rational as he assumes and the parameters of the econometric models used, if properly constructed, would change very slowly, if at all. My explanation for the ready acceptance of the Lucas view by many economists is that by the mid-1970s econometricians in general had failed to build econometric models that were good enough to produce good forecasts. It was not difficult to build low-quality large econometric models by extensive data mining, a practice which Fair (1986) and Chow (1967) tried to avoid. Being disappointed by the majority of econometric models, the profession easily echoed the Lucas complaint. This digression by Lucas aside, it is generally agreed today that the method of optimal control is applicable for the design of optimal economic policies (see, e.g. Woodford (2003)).

Given the possibility of obtaining an optimal feedback rule for the setting of macroeconomic policies, are we to build a suitable macroeconomic model and derive from it optimal control rules (plural because of multiple objective functions, parameter uncertainty, etc.) to recommend to the government officials?

Several considerations should be taken seriously in using the method of optimal control for economic policy recommendation.

It may not be the best to follow my original and somewhat naive idea in the 1970s to make policy recommendations in two steps: first, to find the optimal policy rule using an econometric model, and second, to sell the policy to policymakers.

It may be better to use the government official's objective function than to use our own objective function if we are to help the government official in making the best decision from his point of view. However, there is difficulty in achieving this because, not being technically equipped, a government official may not be convinced that our recommendation will serve to achieve his objective.

A related point is that we need to acquire skills for explaining a result derived from the mathematics of dynamic optimization to a policymaker intuitively and using plain English (or Chinese). This suggestion is more easily said than done, but some economists or researchers are able to communicate verbally the results of their research to intelligent people who do not have the technical-mathematical background.

Related to the last point is the ability to instill confidence on the part of policymakers though successful communication on less technical matters. When the time comes to communicate the results of technical analysis as obtained by dynamic optimization, the friendly official may be willing to be persuaded.

A better approach is to have a collection of good policies rather than just a single optimum policy to recommend. An adviser should find a collection of feasible policies that are improvements over the existing policy. Keep in mind this collection of policies and try to sell one of them to the policymaker. This is like the strategy of a car salesman who has a collection of cars to sell. His mission is accomplished by selling just one car from the collection. Your mission is accomplished by convincing the government official to adopt just one of your policies. Like a car salesman, you can try to sell several proposed policies until one is finally chosen by your customer.

An economist can combine the last two strategies by having a collection of good policies and using his communication skills to explain them to the government officials. Or better still, he should be open-minded enough to let the government officials influence him and teach him that there might be other policies than those in his collection. It was good for both the economic adviser and the government officials to get together to work it out, just like my experience of working with government officials in Taiwan and in the PRC when we learned from each other and worked out the best policy jointly. Thus the optimal control rules from dynamic optimization are only the initial knowledge for solving a policy problem. In the meantime we should be prepared to improve our knowledge by learning from the officials who are seeking our advice. Good policies can be and should be worked out cooperatively and interactively.

5 Implementation of Government Policies

From my study on China's environmental problems and policies, I have learned that even after the government has adopted a certain policy it may not materialize because responsible government officials fail to implement it.

Let me cite a few examples from the Chinese economy. Among the pressing problems arising from rural poverty in China today, a most serious one is the mistreatment of Chinese farmers by local Communist Party officials who have control over the affairs of local villages. Land contracted to farmers has been illegally taken by local officials for urban development without adequate compensation. There is a law that guarantees the right of the farmers to keep the land that is contracted to them but this law has been violated many times, leading to fairly widespread but often unreported demonstrations and unrests by mistreated farmers. The central government could not uphold its policy to protect the farmers because it could not control the local party officials.

In the case of healthcare, after the collapse of the commune system that provided healthcare and other services, many rural residents now receive worse healthcare services than during the late 1970s. This is a major case of failure during the very successful economic reform process in China. In recent years, the central government has tried to institute a medical insurance system for all rural residents. The insurance costs 50 yuan per person per year and the government is willing to pay 40 yuan, equally divided between the central and the local government. However, many farmers still did not enroll in this insurance system as of Spring 2007 mainly because they did not trust the government to actually pay the insurance premium for their benefit. The failure to implement policies for environmental protection is well documented.

Given the importance of implementation, let me suggest that before policy recommendations are made and perhaps even before research to support the policy is completed, problems of implementation should be taken into account. If one knows that a certain policy cannot be implemented, recommending it is useless. As I have suggested before, a policy has to be feasible for us to recommend it. A policy that has no chance of being successfully implemented should be treated as an infeasible policy.

It is equally important to consider the problem of policy implementation in the design of the policy itself. For example, I suggested that if a provincial governor fails to enforce central environmental policies for protecting the environment, he should be subject to severe punishment, including the loss of his position. While making this recommendation I realized that the central government might not have such a strong resolve to adopt the policy that I recommended. However, I considered this recommendation feasible as long as there was some chance for its adoption.

6 Making Social Changes Without Going Through the Government

The discussion in this chapter has concentrated on influencing the government in order to make social changes. There are two other important channels through which social changes take place.

The most important channel is through the market. Social changes are made in a market economy by the actions of many individuals who innovate and by the adoption of their innovations through the market. Major corporations are engaged in research and development, the results of which are sold to the market. Research conducted in universities has resulted in major innovations that have changed the society as well.

A second important point known to economists is expressed well by Keynes, who pointed out that the world is influenced more by men of ideas than by politicians who just follow their ideas. Karl Marx had a great deal of influence on many government officials for decades, whether his ideas are valid or not. My most respected teacher Milton Friedman perhaps had more influence during the second half of the 20th century on the functioning of the American economy and many other economies than any other individual, government officials included. His research has made a tremendous impact on society, particularly in the formulation of monetary policy, the use of vouchers for paying tuition, and the respect of the freedom to choose in many aspects of life. He accomplished this by writing, speaking (on TV or in person) and teaching students.

References

Chow, G. C. "Multiplier, accelerator and liquidity preference in the determination of national income in the United States." *Review of Economics and Statistics*, (Feb 1967): 1–15.

Chow, G. C. "Optimal stochastic control of linear economic systems." *Journal of Money, Credit and Banking*, 2 (1970): 291–302.

Chow, G. C. *Analysis and Control of Dynamic Economic Systems.* New York: John Wiley and Sons, 1975.

Chow, G. C. and Yan Shen. "Money, price level and output in the Chinese Macroeconomy." *Asia-Pacific Journal of Accounting and Economics*, 2 (2006): 91–111.

Fair, Ray C. *Specification, Estimation, and Analysis of Macroeconometric Models.* Cambridge, MA: Harvard University Press, 1984.

Friedman, Milton and Rose Friedman. *Free to Choose: A Personal Statement.* New York: Harcourt Brace Hovanovich, 1979.

Lucas, Robert. "Econometric policy evaluation: A critique." In *The Philip Curve and Labor Markets*, eds. K. Brunner and A. H. Meltzer, 19–46. Amsterdam: North Holland, 1976.

Sims, Christopher. "Macroeconomics and reality." *Econometrica*, 48, 1 (1980): 1–48.

Woodford, Michael. *Interest and Prices: Foundations of a Theory of Monetary Policy.* Princeton: Princeton University Press, 2003.

25

Has China Solved its Population Problem?

Is China's population too large? Let me first consider two possible concerns about a large population. The first is that the food supply is insufficient to feed the Chinese population. China's food production is close to being sufficient to feed its population, but agricultural sufficiency is not necessary. China and other countries which do not produce enough food can always buy it from the world market. The question therefore is whether the world food supply is sufficient to feed the world's population. The answer is definitely yes. In 1798 Thomas Malthus was concerned that because land was limited but population kept on increasing, the food supply would become insufficient. His prediction was wrong because the advance in technology in food production has outpaced the increase in population. Food supply per person today is much higher than in Malthus's time. We can expect a continued increase in food supply per person in the future. Since China's national output has continued to increase, it can afford to increase its food consumption per capita, by buying food from the world market if necessary.

The second is a high population density, or the number of people per unit of land. China's population density is not high. It is not only lower than the population densities in Europe and in Japan but also in Taiwan. In 1980 Taiwan had only 0.12 acre of cultivated cropland per person while mainland China had 0.27 acre.

If China's population is not too large for the above reasons, why should we limit the growth of China's population? One answer is that population growth will reduce the growth of GDP per capita, but this reduction is very small as seen by the following facts. The rate of increase in GDP per capita equals to the rate of increase in total GDP minus the rate of increase in population. Increase in total GDP was about 9.5 percent per year from 1978 to 2000 and has been even higher since 2000. In 1980 the birth rate was 1.82 percent of the population and the death rate was 0.63, giving a natural rate of increase of 1.19 percent that year. In 2004, the birth rate was 1.23, the death rate was 0.64 and the natural rate of increase was 0.59 percent (see Table 1). This shows that any policy to control China's birth rate could reduce the birth rate or the rate of population growth only by about 0.6 percent. A reduction of the rate of growth of GDP per capita by 0.6 percent out of a rate of growth of total GDP of 9.5 percent is very small. China's rapid growth in GDP per capita will not be affected much by a population policy.

Next, I turn to some harmful effects of controlling the birth rate.

1. Having children is an investment in human capital. Just like an investment in building a house for one's own use or for profit in the future, investment in human capital is costly today (in the cost of bearing children) but will yield productive human capital in the future. In building a house, we do not just consider the cost today when we are building it but also the benefit after it is built. The same is true for having children. In a previous article I discussed how important human capital is for China's economic development.

Table 1. Birth rate, death rate and natural rate of population growth.

Year	Birth rate	Death rate	Natural pop growth rate
1978	18.25	6.25	12
1980	18.21	6.34	11.87
1981	20.91	6.36	14.55
1982	22.28	6.6	15.68
1983	20.19	6.9	13.29
1984	19.9	6.82	13.08
1985	21.04	6.78	14.26
1986	22.43	6.86	15.57
1987	23.33	6.72	16.61
1988	22.37	6.64	15.73
1989	21.58	6.54	15.04
1990	21.06	6.67	14.39
1991	19.68	6.7	12.98
1992	18.24	6.64	11.6
1993	18.09	6.64	11.45
1994	17.7	6.49	11.21
1995	17.12	6.57	10.55
1996	16.98	6.56	10.42
1997	16.57	6.51	10.06
1998	15.64	6.5	9.14
1999	14.64	6.46	8.18
2000	14.03	6.45	7.58
2001	13.38	6.43	6.95
2002	12.86	6.41	6.45
2003	12.41	6.4	6.01
2004	12.29	6.42	5.87
2005	12.4	6.51	5.89
2006	12.09	6.81	5.28
2007	12.1	6.93	5.17

2. Related to the above point is the argument that we cannot afford to pay for the education of too many children. This argument is invalid. First, if we need human capital in the future, it is better to have enough even if some will be less educated. Second, just because some families cannot afford to pay for, or are not provided with, good education for their children, we are not justified in limiting all Chinese families from having as many children as they desire. Third, much of the child's education is family education which all Chinese families can provide.
3. The one-child family policy has led to unhealthy development of children. They do not have siblings to grow up with and to learn from. Just by playing together, an older child can teach a younger one more effectively in many situations than the parents can. They also can have fun together.
4. A restrictive population policy has encouraged illegal behavior in rural households. They would kill female children or have several children whom they would hide when officials came to check.
5. Related to the first point is that in the future there will not be enough working people to support an aged population .

Let us find out how the birth rate in China has changed. According to the *China Statistical Yearbook*, the birth rate declined from 34.03 per 1000 persons in 1957, to 23.01 in 1975 and then to 18.25 in 1978 (before the one-child policy was introduced in 1980), rose to 23.33 in 1987 and declined steadily afterwards to 12.86 in 2002. There is an economic explanation for the large drop in birth rate from 1957 to 1978. Labor participation rate in China increased from 32.2 percent in 1957 to 55.2 percent in 1978, mainly because a much larger fraction of women had entered the labor force. Working women had more difficulty in bearing children. There is also an economic explanation for the increase in birth rate between 1980 and 1987 in spite of the one-child family policy. As the rural population became richer after the economic reform in agriculture, they could afford to have more children. The gradual decline in the birth rate in recent years is due to urbanization. In rural areas children are productive and less costly to support. In urban areas the costs of food, lodging and schooling for children are higher and the children are not productive. Hence, when people move from rural areas to cities, the country's birth rate decreases. China after 1987 is an example of this law of economics. From the above facts we understand that the birth rate in China has changed a great deal without the influence of government policy.

Finally, I would like to point out some advantages of having a large population.

1. When a population is larger, it is easier to select the most talented people in all fields. These talented people contribute a great deal to a country's development. In the 2008 Olympic Games, China had an advantage partly because it had a large population from which to select the best athletes for training and for competition.

2. A larger population provides a larger market to attract foreign investment to China. Foreign investors have come to invest in China not only because labor is inexpensive and of good quality. They also want to sell their products in China's domestic market.

3. A larger market is conducive to technological innovations. Innovations of new and better products are costly. Unless there is a large market to sell the new products, it would not be economical to innovate.

4. A country with a larger population has more influence in world affairs, other things being equal.

I therefore support the current policy to loosen the control on births in China. Parents who were the only child have been allowed to have two children. I understand that a policy is being considered to allow all families to have two children in the future. These are encouraging signs. From the discussion above,

I believe that we can relax the control on population in China even more. As urbanization takes place and as women have better working opportunities, the birth rate will naturally decline. This has already happened in China as it has happened in other countries during the course of economic development. Countries like Japan and Singapore have found their population to be too small and need to encourage families to have more children. If population growth is controlled too strictly today, in the future the working population in China will be too small to sustain healthy economic development.

26

The Problem of Rural Poverty in China

This paper describes the economic conditions of rural China regarding poverty. By dividing the problem of rural poverty into three components, it explains why rural poverty is China's number one economic problem in spite of the significant improvement in the living standard of the rural population. After discussing the solution proposed by the Chinese government, it raises two policy questions, one concerning a proposal to eliminate the operational functions of township governments in streamlining the local government structure and the second on the possibility of controlling the abuse of power by local party officials that infringes on the rights of the farmers. A comparison with the conditions in India is provided.

1 Introduction

China's rapid economic growth in the order of 9.4 percent per year since economic reform started in 1978 is well recognized. Many observers also agree that the momentum for further growth in the foreseeable future is assured.

The large amount of wealth created and the insufficient attention given to the welfare of residents in the rural regions have created a large income gap between the urban rich and rural poor as well as opportunities of exploitation of the latter by local government and Communist Party officials. Hence the country's leaders now consider the top economic and social problem to be rural poverty despite the substantial improvement in the living standard of the rural population in recent years.

In Section 2 of this paper, I will examine the economic conditions of the rural population, its absolute improvement, its relative status as compared with the urban population and the increase in disparity in per capita consumption between regions. In Section 3, I will divide the problem of rural poverty into three components and explain why it is the number one problem in spite of the improvement in the economic conditions of the poor. Section 4 is a description of government policy to solve the rural poverty problem. Section 5 discusses two policy issues concerning the government's solution, one on the policy to eliminate the functions of township governments in five years and the second on the protection of farmers' rights to keep the land contracted to them. Section 6 is a brief discussion of the poverty problem in India by comparison. Section 7 concludes.

2 Statistics on Rural Poverty and Economic Disparity in China

In this section I examine three kinds of statistics on rural poverty and economic disparity in China. One is the means of per capita disposable income and per capita consumption of urban and rural residents and their rates of change. The second is the change in the lower tail of income distribution of rural residents through time. The third is measures of dispersion of per capita income or consumption across provinces.

2.1 Trends of per capita income and consumption of urban and rural residents

Table 1 shows annual per capita disposable income of urban and rural residents. The ratio of urban to rural per capita income decreased from 2.57 in 1978 to 1.86 in 1985, showing the initial benefits of agricultural reform through the household responsibility system of assigning land to individual farm households. However, the ratio increased in favor of the urban residents afterwards, rising steadily from the late 1980s to 2003 when it reached 3.23. Thus, income disparity between urban and rural residents has increased steadily since the mid-1980s.

Concerning the improvement of per capita income in real terms for the rural residents, we record the consumer price index for rural residents in the last row of Table 1 which shows an increase from 100.0 in 1985 to 320.2 in 2003. In 2003 prices, the per capita income of rural residents in 1989 was 602(3.202/1.579) or 1220.8 yuan. This amounts to an exponential rate of increase from 1989 to 2003 of (ln2622–ln1220.8)/14 or 0.0546 per year, or by 5.61 percent per year, a fairly substantial rate of increase. A similar calculation for urban residents shows per capita real income increased from

Table 1. Annual per capita disposable income of urban and rural residents (yuan).

Year	1978	1980	1985	1989	1997	2002	2003
Urban	343.4	477.6	739.1	1374	5160	7703	8472
Rural	133.6	191.3	397.6	602	2090	2476	2622
Income ratio	2.570	2.497	1.859	2.282	2.469	3.111	3.231
Urban CPI	100.0	109.5	134.2	219.2	481.9	475.1	479.4
Rural CPI	–	–	100.0	157.9	322.3	315.2	320.2

Source: *China Statistical Yearbook 1999*, Table 10.1 for years up to 1985; *China Statistical Yearbook 2004*, Table 10-1 for income data beginning 1989, Table 9-2 for the urban and rural consumer price indices (respectively with 1978 = 100 and 1985 = 100).

Table 2. Annual per capita living expenditure of urban and rural households (yuan).

Year	1989	1997	2002	2003
Urban	1211	4186	6030	6511
Rural	515	1617	1834	1943
Ratio	2.351	2.589	3.288	3.351

Source: China Statistical Yearbook 2004, Table 10-1.

1374(479.4/219.2) = 3005.0 yuan in 2003 prices in 1989 to 8472 yuan, implying an exponential rate of increase of (ln8472–ln3005)/14 = 0.0740, which is two percentage points higher than the rural figure.

On per capita consumption, Table 2 provides the annual per capita living expenditure of urban and rural households for 1989, 1997, 2002 and 2003. The ratio of urban to rural expenditure increased from 2.351 in 1989 to 3.351 in 2003, showing a very large increase similar to the increase in the income ratio in Table 1.

In 1989, real per capita consumption in 2003 prices for rural residents was 515(320.2/157.9) = 1044.4 yuan. This gives an average exponential rate of increase of (ln1943–ln1044.4)/14 = 0.04434 from 1989 to 2003, a very high rate of increase by comparison with other developing countries. In 1989, real per capita consumption in 2003 prices for urban residents was 1211(479.4/219.2) = 2648.5 yuan. This implies an average exponential rate of increase of (ln6511–ln2648.5)/14 = 0.06425 from 1989 to 2003, also two percentage points higher than for rural residents.

Thus the data show that the urban–rural income and consumption disparity has increased, but that rural residents have enjoyed a fairly substantial rate of increase in both income and consumption, to the order of 5.5 and 4.5

percent per year respectively, even though these are two percentage points below the corresponding figures for urban residents.

There are some other aspects of consumption not measured in the above statistics on per capita consumption expenditure. First, per capita education expenditure provided by the government for urban residents was higher than for rural residents. Second, land was available for rural residents to build their own houses. As a result, the living space per person available for rural residents in their own housing was more than the housing space for urban residents for many years. Third, medical care for urban residents provided by the government under an insurance system was better than that for rural residents. Only 22.5 percent of rural residents are covered by the rural cooperative medical care insurance system while the vast majority of urban residents receive adequate medical care, with some 80 percent of medical resources concentrated in cities. In terms of infrastructure, the supply of running water is less adequate in rural areas. More than 60 percent of rural households do not have access to flush toilets. Six percent of villages are still beyond the reach of highways. Two percent of villages have no electricity supply. Six percent of villages do not have telephones. Some 150 million rural households face problems in fuel supply. However, incorporating these elements of consumption will not affect the general conclusions reached above concerning the urban–rural comparison of per capita income and consumption.

2.2 Percentage of rural residents with per capita income below the poverty line

Since the poverty problem may not be a problem among all rural residents but among the poorest of them, we have provided in Table 3 the left tail of the per capita annual income distribution of the rural residents. If we draw the poverty line in 2003 as having an income below 600 yuan, we find 3.47 percent below it, or about 28 million out of a rural population of 800 million, still a substantial number of people. (The 28 million figure is consistent

Table 3. Percentage of rural households in different income ranges.

Income	1980	1985	1990	1995	2000	2002	2003
< 100	9.80	0.96	0.30	0.21	0.31	0.40	0.49
100–200	51.80	11.26	1.78	0.36	0.20	0.19	0.18
200–300	25.30	25.61	6.56	0.78	0.43	0.28	0.31
300–400	8.60	24.00	12.04	1.47	0.69	0.50	0.52
400–500	2.90	15.85	14.37	2.30	1.01	0.79	0.78
500–600	–	9.06	13.94	3.37	1.37	1.25	1.19
600–800	–	8.02	20.80	9.54	4.44	3.62	3.25
< 800	98.4	94.76	69.79	18.03	8.45	7.03	6.72
< 600	98.4	86.74	48.99	15.21	4.01	3.41	3.47
< 500	–	–	–	11.84	2.64	2.16	2.28

with the official statement in 2005 that 26 million rural people are living in poverty and nearly 20 million urban people are living on the government's minimum allowance). In 1990 when the rural CPI was about half of the 2003 CPI, the percentage of households with per capita income below 300 yuan was 8.64. In 1985, when the CPI was about a third, the percentage of households with per capita income below 200 was 12.22 percent. Thus the percentage of rural population remaining below the poverty line of 600 yuan in 2003 prices has decreased substantially from 12 percent in 1985 to 9 percent in 1990 and to 3.5 percent in 2003. In 1985, the Chinese farmers were by and large happy, as their economic conditions had improved significantly after the introduction of the household responsibility system of private farming.

2.3 Inequality in wealth distribution

The third kind of statistics we examine is the distribution of income across provinces by considering the standard deviation of the natural logarithm of rural consumption expenditure per capita, treating consumption as a measure of permanent income or wealth. In 1981 this standard deviation computed for the 28 provinces then in existence was 0.2612, as compared with 0.3475 in 1998 for the same 28 provinces (see Chow, 2002, p. 169). Thus consumption inequality among provinces increased between these two years, at the average rate of (0.3475–0.2612)/17 = 0.00508 or about half a percentage point per year. To see whether the increase in consumption disparity has slowed down, I have computed the same standard deviation for 1993, using data on p. 281 of *China Statistical Yearbook 1994*, and obtained 0.3370. The average rate of increase in the standard deviation in the five years from 1993 to 1998 is (0.3475–0.3370)/5 = 0.0021, much lower than 0.00508. Thus the rate of increase in disparity slowed down in the late 1990s but was still in the range of two tenths of one percent per year. The same standard deviation for 2004 is 0.3731 (based on data in *China Statistical Yearbook 2005*, Table 10–26 for the same 28 provinces), suggesting that the increase in dispersion has continued between 1998 and 2004 at the average rate of (0.3731-0.3475)/6 = 0.0064 per year. This agrees with the continued increase in income disparity up to the present as found in Section 2.1 and shows in addition that the rate of increase in disparity was even higher in the last six years from 1998 to 2004 than in the five years from 1993 to 1998 and also in the 17 years between 1981 and 1998 (with possible errors due to the omission of Hainan, Chongqing and Tibet in the calculations for 1998 and 2004).

A related question is whether rural per capita consumption increased in the poorest provinces and at what rate. From Chow (2002, Table 9.2), the three provinces with the lowest consumption in 1981 were Gansu, Yunnan and Qinghai, with per capita rural consumption of 135.23, 137.75 and 141.68 respectively. From Chow (2002, Table 9.5), in 1998 these three provinces had per capita rural consumption of 939.55, 1312.31 and 1117.79 yuan. The general retail price index given in Table 9–2 of *China Statistical Yearbook 1999* is 110.7 in 1981, 128.1 in 1985 and 370.9 in 1998; the general consumer price index for rural areas is 100.0 in 1985 and 319.1 in 1998. To approximate the increase in consumer prices for rural areas, we assume the same proportional increase in these two indices between 1981 and 1985 to obtain a value of 86.4 for the latter index in 1981. The increase between 1981 and 1998 in rural consumer prices from 86.4 to 319.1 is a factor of 3.69. The increase in the nominal value of per capita consumption is 939.55/135.23 = 6.95 for Gansu, 9.81 for Yunan and 7.89 for Qinghai. If we consider the two other poorest provinces as of 1998 among the original 28, namely Shanxi and Guizhou, with consumption per capita of 1056.45 and 1094.39, and consider their improvement from the 1981 values of 147.78 and 162.51 in Chow (1992, Table 9.2), we find factors of 7.15 and 6.73. Thus Guizhou is the province with the smallest increase in rural consumption per capita between 1981 and 1998. The improvement in real consumption during this period is only a factor of 6.73/3.69 or 1.82. In terms of exponential rate of increase per year between 1981 and 1998, Guizhou experienced a rate of 0.035.

To summarize our discussion on disparity as measured by the dispersion in rural consumption per capita among provinces, the disparity has increased at the rate of about half a percentage point per year between 1981 and 1998, but the rate of increase has slowed down to 0.2 of a percentage point in the last five years of this period. There have been significant increases in the level of real consumption per capita in all provinces in the meantime. Even Guizhou, the province with the slowest rate of increase among the original 28 provinces, experienced an average exponential rate of increase of 0.035 per year.

3 Three Components of the Problem of Rural Poverty

I have divided the problem of rural poverty into the following three components:

The first is the income gap between the urban and rural residents. From the data presented in the previous section, it is clear that the problem of rural poverty is not due to the low income level of the rural population, nor to a small rate of increase in income. Per capita income of rural residents has increased fairly rapidly, in the order of 5.5 percent per year since 1989, and the percentage of rural residents with income below the poverty line has declined rapidly. It is true that the gap in per capita income between the urban and rural residents has widened but the rate of increase for the latter has been so rapid that the rural population, on average or as judged by the poorest among them, is so much better off economically than before. If one uses income as the sole measure of rural poverty, the problem has to be viewed either as (1) the deterioration of the *relative* income of the rural residents in spite of the rapid increase in absolute income or (2) the possible social discontent created during a period of improvement in income level which enables the poor to express their discontent. These two interpretations explain part of the problem of rural poverty but are not sufficient to explain the seriousness of the current problem which is accounted for by the following two components.

The second component is the unfavorable treatment by the central government towards the rural residents as compared with the urban residents. The inadequacy of government provision for the rural residents will be detailed in Section 4 when government policy to remedy the situation is discussed. First, the government has spent less on infrastructure investment in rural areas than in urban areas. It invested only a limited amount to improve agricultural productivity. Second, it provided less welfare benefits including healthcare and education subsidies to rural residents. Although much labor mobility was allowed for farmers to move to urban areas to find work, those working in urban areas are subject to discrimination under the government policy (introduced in the 1950s) of distinguishing between the residence status and thus the entitled benefits of the urban and rural populations. The migrating workers do not have residence permits in the cities and cannot receive the services provided such as healthcare and schooling for their children. Third, although the commune system was abolished, procurement of farm products by government agencies has continued and the procurement prices are often set below market prices. In the meantime the farmers are not allowed to sell their products to private traders as private trading and transportation of grain are prohibited. Thus the market economy does not function in the distribution and pricing of grain for the benefit of the farmers.

The neglect of the central government in dealing with the rural problems is probably not by design but a result of the historical development of economic reform. The initial success of the privatization of farming in the early 1980s that improved the economic conditions of farmers was a result of market forces at work and not of government intervention. The strategy of "letting some people get rich first" resulted in the income gap between the urban and rural population. The historical entitlement of welfare benefits provided to the urban population who had the required residence permits excluded the rural population – this was inherited from the period of economic planning, not a new policy favoring the urban population, while the collapse of the commune system took away similar welfare benefits to the rural population. Finally, the need to deal with other important reform problems concerning the state enterprises, the banking and financial system, and the open-door policy, together with the human and financial resources required to accomplish them (including resources for building infrastructure in the special economic zones as part of the open-door policy), has also contributed to the neglect of the rural population. When the Chinese government realized the seriousness of the relative poverty problem facing the farmers, perhaps valuable time had been lost. This is called the *san nong* (three rural) problem, covering farming, rural areas and farmers.

The third, and very important, component of the *san nong* problem is that farmers' rights have been violated by the illegal activities of local government officials. This component is not poverty in the narrow sense of low income *per se* but is concerned with the economic welfare of the low-income farmers when their property rights are violated. The most disconcerting example is the confiscation of land from farmers for urban development while many farmers receive a compensation that is arbitrary and well below market price. Second, many farmers and other rural residents are not paid, or not paid on time, for work performed such as public works and teaching in public schools. Third, farmers are subject to illegal levies. The levies include the increase in tax on the reported acreage of the farmer's land over the acreage actually used, special tax for growing commercial crops aside from grain and livestock feed, fees for schools, road construction and other services provided by the local government. One reason for the extra levies is the tax reform of 1994 which increased the proportion of government revenue paid to the central government (from 22.0 percent in 1993 to 55.7 percent in 2004) at the expense of provincial and local governments. Another reason is the central government's policy to assign the responsibility of providing nine years of "compulsory education" and adequate healthcare to local governments.

Concerning the violation of the farmers' right to the use and transfer of land, a Chinese official in charge of rural policy Chen Xiwen (2006, p. 37) writes:

> It is stipulated in our Constitution that in rural China ... land is collectively owned by farmers but contracted to individual households. However, at the grassroots level, few officials have read this provision ... Therefore, some grassroots officials constantly make trouble with farmers' land, causing endless land contract conflicts. Because of this, the Rural Land Contract Law was passed in March 2003 in which there are two basic regulations: (1) during the contract period, the contract granting party shall not be allowed to take back the contracted land; and (2) during the contract period, the contract-granting party shall not be allowed to adjust the contracted land. Neither regulation, however, has been well implemented.

As head of the Institute for the Study of the *San Nong* Problem of the Central Party School, Zeng Yesong (2004, p. 43) states the problem of the lack of basic rights on the part of Chinese farmers as follows:

> Farmers in many places have limited right to information. Policies of the central government fail to reach the farmers. In some provinces policy documents to reduce taxes on farmers were not distributed to them. In some

> places, farmers were mistreated because the matter was not handled on time. They even suffered from subjugation which forced them to report to authorities above. However, many people in the government above believed only in the officials below and not in the farmers. They found small excuse to imprison the farmers, and even persecute those who dared to report to officials above. This not only deprives the farmers of their right to speak out but also interferes with their human rights.

In a popular book, well-known Chinese authors Chen and Wu (2005, pp. 108–9) provide a dramatic illustration of the extortion of illegal levies in a village. The village Party secretary led a group of several armed tax collectors to each house to collect a "school construction fee" of six yuan when all school buildings were in good condition. When one housewife did not have the money to pay, the collectors took away a television set. After returning home and finding out about this incident, the husband was brave enough to visit the county Party secretary to file a complaint but he was ignored. When the village Party secretary found out, he went back to the house for a second time to take away a bicycle. This story illustrates the lawlessness and abuse of power of local Party officials, and that the *san nong* problem is not due to extreme poverty at least in this case since the farm household had a television set and a bicycle but due to the violation of the farmers' rights.

Throughout much of Chinese history, local government officials considered themselves a class above the farmers, with the authority to rule over them. The abuse of power under the PRC is worse because the officials are given even more power to control the activities of the citizens. Some well-publicized stories of the abuse of power by local Party and government officials are documented in Chen and Wu (2005), which also describes the multi-level bureaucracy in the village-township-country governments that protect each other's interests and positions and fail to carry out policies of the central government to benefit the farmers. This is a point also stated in Zeng (2004, p. 43) quoted above. Chapter 1 of Chen and Wu (2005) tells the story of citizens of a village sending representatives to report to the country officials the illegal levies and false financial accounting by village officials, who later mistreated one of the representatives, sent policemen to put him to jail and eventually beat him to death (though perhaps not intentionally). This story corroborates Zeng's (2004, p. 43) account of the violation of farmers' human rights by local government and Party officials.

The abuse of power by local officials is known to be fairly widespread, as stated in the writings of the three authors quoted above and evidenced by the large number of demonstrations and protests by farmers reported in the news media. Zhang (2006, pp. 19–20) quoted (1) statistics provided by Han (2003) that some 34 million farmers have lost their land to local government land-taking and (2) statistics provided by the Ministry of Construction to show that, between January and June 2004, 4,026 groups and 18,620 individuals had lodged petitions over allegedly illicit land confiscations, compared to 3,929 groups and 18,071 individuals for the entire year of 2003.

4 Solution Proposed by the Chinese Government

Realizing these problems the central government has given the agriculture sector much attention in recent years. In 1993, the "*san nong* policy" was introduced to improve agricultural productivity in farming, promote economic development of rural areas and increase the income of farmers. It includes increasing capital investment in rural areas and helping farmers to use better technology and better methods for farming, reducing corruption and misbehavior of local government officials and providing economic assistance to farmers. The development of the agricultural sector was the first important task mentioned in Premier Zhu Rongji's work report of March 2001 to the National People's Congress.

In February 2004, the State Council announced a set of policies to improve the living conditions of farmers that include the following:

1. Support the development of agricultural production in grain producing areas to increase the incomes of farmers. This includes providing incentives to farmers, improving methods of production as well as the quality of land, and increasing government investment in agriculture.
2. Change the structure of agricultural production by improving output mix, management and technology.
3. Develop industrial and service industries in rural areas, including the encouragement of township and village as well as private enterprises. (Township and village enterprises, perhaps involving less capital than those that flourished in the 1980s and of a more primitive nature that is tied to agricultural production, did not develop in the very poor regions probably because of lack of human capital among residents and lack of incentives on the part of local government officials to promote them.)
4. Assist the farmers in moving to urban areas to find work by reducing various levies collected from them by city governments and by giving responsibility to the latter for the training of the incoming farmers and for the education of their children.
5. Establish market mechanisms for the distribution and marketing of grain by allowing more distribution channels, including collectives, and by the promotion of farm products.
6. Build infrastructure for rural areas, including water supply, roads and electricity in poor areas.
7. Carry out reform in rural areas including the tax system.

8. Continue to improve programs to reduce poverty by subsidies and other means.
9. Strengthen the leadership of the Communist Party in putting the above policies into practice.

One important step was taken in 2005 when the central government decided to abolish all taxes on farmers. This policy seemed to be a good move if one compared the costs and benefits of taxing farmers. The benefits were small since such taxes accounted for just over one percent of total government revenue. The costs of taxing farmers were much larger, as the tax increased their discontent which might lead to social instability and provided an excuse for local government officials to impose illegal levies. Although some local officials might continue to impose such levies, the policy of not taxing farmers makes it more difficult for them to do so.

On February 21, 2006, and for three consecutive years (according to *People's Daily Online* on February 23, 2006) the Central Committee of the Chinese Communist Party and the State Council issued its most important "Number 1 Document" on the subject of agriculture, farmers and countryside development. This document is more comprehensive and systematic than the previous two. Agriculture and rural areas are to receive higher fractions of national fiscal spending, budgetary investment on fixed assets and credits. In 2005, over 300 billion yuan (37.5 billion US dollars) from the budget of the central government was allocated to support rural development, a 50 percent increase from the 2002 figure when the price level was stable. In addition to direct financial support, the government announced the abolition of agricultural tax as of January 1, 2006, which totaled 22 billion yuan (2.75 billion US dollars) in the previous year. The evolution of government policies to deal with the *san nong* problem between 2004 and 2006 illustrates the use of experimentation and observation in revising and improving policies, termed "crossing the river by feeling the rocks" by China's reform leader Deng Xiaoping.

The 2006 Number 1 Document covers:

1. Infrastructure building that will include the provision of safe drinking water, clean energy supply (by the use of methane, straw gasification technology, small hydropower, solar energy, wind farms and upgrading of power grids) and the construction of country roads.
2. A national support system for agriculture and farmers consisting of:
    (a) direct subsidies to grain production (to be raised to 50 percent of the grain risk fund used to stabilize market price) and to grain farmers for the purchase of high-quality seeds and farm machinery;
    (b) improvement of agricultural production and marketing;
    (c) facilitating the migration of rural labor by removing discriminative restrictions on migrant workers in urban job markets and gradually providing them with a social security system, possibly with a guarantee of subsistence allowances in rural areas (insurance for occupational injuries to cover all migrant workers);
    (d) increase in funding for the rural compulsory education system, and reduction or exemption of tuition for students included in the system in western areas, to be extended to all rural areas;
    (e) the training of farmers to make them well-educated and technologically literate with basic knowledge in management, with 100 million to be trained by 2010, including 50 million in agricultural technology and another 50 million in other sectors;
    (f) a social assistance program covering 50 million people and four areas (regular social assistance providing minimum living subsidies to poor urban and rural residents, emergency assistance for people suffering from disasters, temporary assistance for low-income migrants to

urban areas, and social assistance from donations, with the total assistance amounting to only 0.02 percent of GDP);

(g) more financial support for the new rural cooperative healthcare system (since rural residents, who account for some 60 percent of the nation's total population, only have access to 20 percent of the country's medical resources) both from the central and local fiscal systems in 2006, to cover almost all the rural areas in 2008. The plan is to cover 40 percent of China's counties in a new government-backed medicare cooperative program for farmers in 2006, and to promote the program to all rural areas in the next few years. Under the plan the government will allocate 40 yuan to every account of farmers who pay ten yuan each, and set up a clinic in every village in the near future;

(h) rural financial reform of community financial institutions in order to provide agricultural insurance and easily accessible loans to rural households and small and medium business enterprises.

3. Streamlining the functions of the multi-level government system (central, provincial, country, township and village) by elimination of the operational functions of township governments within five years and in the interim changing their functions from engaging in the investment and operation of their own projects and production of grain to creating a favorable environment for the farmers, while the finance of countries will be placed under the direct control of the provincial governments or of the villages themselves.

4. Village planning that is environmentally friendly, by remodeling existing houses rather than constructing new ones, efficient use of land, energy and materials for the construction of farm housing and the preservation of ancient villages and residence.

The *san nong* policies announced above were incorporated in the 11th Five-Year Plan passed by the National People's Congress on March 14, 2006, under the heading of "building a new socialist countryside" and "according to the requirement of advanced production, improved livelihood, a civilized social atmosphere, clean and tidy villages and democratic administration." The budget allocated for these policies amounted to 339.7 billion yuan from the central government in 2006 as compared with 297.5 billion yuan from the central government budget in 2005 spent on agriculture, rural areas and farmers, the latter being an increase of 34.9 billion yuan from 2004.

In summary, the policies of the central government aim mainly at redirecting economic resources to the rural areas (items 1 and 2 listed above) and also at streamlining the structure of local governments (item 3).

5 Two Policy Issues in the Solution of the Chinese Government

This section raises two questions concerning the solution of the Chinese government outlined above, one on streamlining the local government structure and the second on the possibility of enforcing a policy to solve the third component of the *san nong* problem.

The first question is concerned with item 3 of the 2006 Number 1 Document: to streamline the multi-level local government structure by eliminating the operational functions of township governments in five years. The main purpose of this policy is to eliminate the taxation power of local governments at both the country and the township levels and thus to reduce the opportunity and power for corruption on the part of country and township level government officials. However there may be difficulties in implementing this policy. Township governments have been in existence for many years and played an important role in recent Chinese history. Taking the form of communes before economic reform, they provided healthcare and education and directed construction projects for the rural population. In the 1980s and early 1990s they established township and village enterprises that propelled China's rapid economic growth. A number of questions can be raised concerning the policy to eliminate township governments in five years and to take away the financial authority of country officials.

Where would the township government officials go five years from now? Supposedly some are due to retire and others will work in departments of the country governments above. In the interim, if they are not allowed to operate enterprises, how would they find sufficient financing for their government and what incentive would they have to create a favorable environment for the farmers as they are supposed to do? Why should they be treated differently from other government officials and even university administrators who are allowed to operate enterprises to generate additional income for their units and even for themselves? Resistance by officials in township governments whose power is being taken away and by officials in country governments whose financial authority is being taken away may present a serious obstacle to the implementation of this policy. These are natural questions to ask when such a bold move is proposed to change the local government structure. I assume that the Chinese leadership has considered these questions carefully and found solutions to them. It will be interesting to observe the implementation of this policy in the next five years.

The second issue concerning the official solution is the absence of any provision to deal with the third component of the *san nong* problem, namely, to protect the rights of farmers to keep the land contracted to them, to be free from illegal taxation and to receive wage payments due to them. In fact, illegal land seizure is the major course of rural discontent. The government is certainly aware of this problem as stated in Chen (2006, p. 37) quoted above. As pointed out earlier, the National People's Congress passed the Rural Land Contract Law in 2003 which stipulates that during the contract period the contract-granting party shall not be allowed to take back the contracted land or to adjust the contracted land. However, the local officials who confiscated the land for economic development disobeyed this law. The strict enforcement of this law is therefore essential. As Premier Wen Jiabao stated on March 14, 2006, strict enforcement of existing policy must be strengthened to protect the farmers' rights at a time when illegitimate land seizures have fueled protests in the countryside (see *New York Times*, March 14, 2006, p. A5).

Therefore, the problem of illegal land seizure boils down to a problem of law enforcement. It can be considered a special case of the problem of corruption when a Party or government official takes advantage of his economic or political power to extract payment from the Chinese people. The extent of this case of corruption, just like corruption in general, increases when the official has more power relative to the people being exploited and when the economic gain is higher. The degree of discontent increases when the exploited are poor and cannot afford to pay. In the present case, the extent of economic abuse is large because the peasants have very little power relative to the village Party secretary and the economic gain in using the land for economic development can be great. There is much discontent because many farmers are poor and cannot afford to give up their land without adequate compensation.

From the above observations, the problem of land seizure will become less serious if farmers have more power to protect themselves or if the Party secretary is deprived of his power to extract money from farmers, and if the economic gain from land seizure is reduced. The degree of discontent will be reduced as farmers get richer. If rural economic development succeeds, farmers will become richer; they will have more power to protect themselves and they can more easily afford to give up their land with less compensation. The local government officials will also have more revenue from taxation but they may desire and be able to extract even more as the price of land goes up.

A key to the solution of this law enforcement problem lies in the ability to take away the power of village Party secretaries to exploit the farmers economically. The leadership in the central government and in the Communist Party has difficulty in disciplining the rank-and-file Party members who have established power locally, as shown by the failure to control the widespread corruption in China (see Chow, 2006, for a discussion of corruption). This explains partly why an explicit policy to discipline the local Party officials is not a part of the No. 1 Document in dealing with the *san nong* problem. Instead, the government's approach to protecting the farmers' rights is to extend democracy in rural areas and to organize farmers' associations for self-protection, as stated in the 11th Five-Year Plan and in Zeng (2004, p. 338). The possible shortcomings of this policy are the following. First, building democracy at the grassroots level will take too long for the solution of the current *san nong* problem which is urgent. Second, providing law and order is a responsibility of the government and should not be relegated to the people's associations. Third, if currently elected village heads are not able to protect the farmers' rights, how can we expect future elected officials to do so?

An effective policy to enforce the law to protect the farmers' rights can be made up of two parts. The first part is a stricter discipline to be applied to Party officials who have violated farmers' rights to land use (or rights to compensation for unpaid wages and for illegal tax levies) and failed to provide them with suitable compensation, together with a commitment of central government to compensate by using its own funds if the local government fails to do so. In 2005, about 45,000 Party members were expelled for misbehavior. The present case of abuse of power can be treated as a most serious offense leading to the loss of Party membership. Since public democratic elections in Chinese villages are widespread, an offending Party secretary can be replaced by the elected village head to serve as the chairman of the most powerful village committee. There are sufficient funds in the central government budget of 340 billion yuan in 2006 allocated for solving the *san nong* problem to set up a guarantee, during the next few years and in cases where the local governments fail, to compensate the deserving farmers among the 34 million who lost their land.

The second part is to allow the news media to report cases of abuse to a larger extent than is the case at present. To implement the above policy of applying strict discipline, a major requirement is to be able to identify cases of abuse. There are two channels to accomplish this. First, the local courts can identify possible cases of violation that are brought to their attention. Second, the farmers can appeal to the news media if it has sufficient freedom to publish cases of violation of farmers' rights. At the present time, such freedom is restricted. It is recognized that in China the degree of freedom given to the news media is a very important matter for the Party leadership to decide on. However, if the leadership desires to solve the third and very important component of the *san nong*, problem it has to allow more freedom for the press to report cases of abuse openly. If the court realizes the existence of both parts of the proposed policy stated above, it would tend to be fair in deciding on what the farmer deserves in each case.

One might be concerned that this policy could lead to numerous farmers filing illegitimate claims, but this is unlikely to happen. Ordinary farmers are in no position to file an illegitimate claim against the more powerful Party officials; they would assert their rights only when injustice is done to them. Furthermore the news media and the courts will render judgments and the farmers in general do not dare to take the risk of filing illegitimate claims. If the claims turn out to be too numerous to handle, one solution would be to settle them in an order based on the claimant's income, with the cases of the poorest farmers to be resolved first.

The announcement of such a policy would boost the confidence of the farmers and the Chinese people in general in the central government and would help alleviate the problem of social discontent in rural China. The determined execution of this policy would also set an example of the central government's ability to eliminate one aspect of corruption. The problem of corruption as a whole is not easy to solve but the successful exercise of discipline in one specific and important case would serve as a first step forward in reducing the degree of corruption. This policy could be an important addition to the policies announced by the State Council on February 21, 2006, as stated above.

Why is such a policy not a part of the 2006 No. 1 Document? Perhaps the central leadership recognizes that the violation of farmers' rights as stated has occurred partly because local government officials need to finance economic development and other responsibilities such as the provision of compulsory education and healthcare that were assigned to them by the central government itself. If this is the case, the central government should provide more funds for such local programs, as it is currently doing to some extent, but in no case should it allow lawless behavior to spread widely. Preserving law and order is a very important function of the Chinese government and should be on top of its list of priorities. Although one cannot expect that the above policy to enforce an important law to protect the rights of farmers will be implemented successfully in all parts of China within one or two years, its successful implementation in substantial parts of rural areas within several years will be a great step forward in solving a very important component of the *san nong* problem and in "building a new socialist countryside" in China.

6 Comparison with India

When we compare the problem of rural poverty in China with that of India, three important propositions can be made. First, China has made much progress in solving its economic problem of poverty as compared with India. Second, in India the problem of income inequality and relative rural poverty does not exist because there has been no rapid economic growth in certain regions, at least until 2003. Third, the abuse of power by local officials and the resulting discontent of the rural population is not a serious problem in India. I will elaborate on these statements below.

Table 4 (see www.indiastat.com) shows the fraction of rural and urban population below the poverty line in selected years in India. The data support our first statement by showing the large fractions of both the rural and urban population remaining below the poverty line in 1999–2000 and the fairly slow reduction in these fractions through the years, in contrast with the statistics shown in Table 3. Since the contrasts in the data are so great, the statement is valid even if the definition of the poverty line is different for the two countries. Second, if this fraction is used to measure income status (instead of mean income) there does not exist a large income gap between the rural and urban population as it does in China. Note that the fraction below the poverty line for the urban population is only slightly smaller than for the rural

Table 4. Incidence of poverty in India.

Population below poverty line (as per expert group methodology) in India (1973–1974, 1977–1978, 1983, 1987–1988, 1993–1994 and 1999–2000)

Sector	1973–74	1977–78	1983	1978–88	1993–94	1999–2000
Population in Millions						
Rural	261.3	264.3	252	231.9	244	193.2
Urban	60	64.6	70.9	75.2	76.3	67
Total	321.3	328.9	322.9	307.1	320.3	260.2
Poverty Ratio (%)						
Rural	56.4	53.1	45.7	39.1	37.3	27.1
Urban	49.0	45.2	40.8	38.2	32.4	23.6
Total	54.9	51.3	44.5	38.9	36.0	26.1

Source: Rural Development Statistics 2002–03, National Institute of Rural Development.
Note: Period of fiscal year in India is April to March, e.g. year shown as 1990–91 relates to April 1990 to March 1991.

population. As of 1999–2000 India was still a very poor country as judged by the large fractions (27.1 percent for rural and 23.6 percent for urban) of its population below poverty line.

As is well-known, India did not experience rapid economic development between 1978 and 2000. This is seen by the fairly slow reduction in the fraction of population below the poverty line and by the relatively small rates of growth, relative to China, of India's per capita net state domestic product (NSDP) in constant prices in recent years as shown in Table 5. From the *World Development Indicator* database, one finds that for the year 2004, China's per capita GDP was 5,495 in PPP (international $) while India's was merely 3,115, showing that China has gone much further in its development path than India.

On the third statement that the abuse of power is primarily a Chinese problem, one can cite a number of factors specific to China. As pointed out earlier, the abuse of power by local officials who consider themselves rulers over the peasants has its roots in Chinese history and the power has increased with the authority given to them by the PRC government. The peasants now have higher incomes and more economic resources, including the right to use public land, creating opportunities for the bureaucrats to exploit. If the economy were not rapidly growing, the market value of the land for use in urban development would be much lower and less worthy of illegal confiscation. All these factors do not exist in India.

Table 5. Growth of per capita NSDP at 1993–1994 prices in india (As on 30.11.2004) from 1994–5 to 2003–4.

Year	1994–1995	1995–1996	1996–1997	1997–1998	1998–1999	1999–2000	2000–2001	2001–2002	2002–2003	2003–2004
India	4.9	5.2	6.1	2.6	4.4	4.3	2.4	4.5	1.8	6.5

Source: Central Statistical Organization (see www.indiastat.com).

7 Conclusion

In this paper I have examined three kinds of statistics on rural poverty and suggested that the problem of rural poverty has three components: income disparity, policy neglect of the central Party and government leadership and violation of the rights of farmers by local party officials. After studying the proposed solution of the government, I have raised one set of questions concerning the possible difficulties in the implementation of the government policy to take away the taxation power of country governments, to eliminate the operational functions of township governments in five years and in the interim not to allow them to operate enterprises as they have been accustomed to do. I have also suggested a policy to protect the rights of farmers to the use of land contracted to them, to compensate them for the illegal seizure of their land by severe punishment of Party officials who violate these rights and by exposing the violations by giving the news media more freedom. Although the solution of the *san nong* problem may take some years, economic forces will naturally enrich the farmers in the future as in the past, if social discontent does not seriously interrupt the economic process under a government policy that protects the basic rights of the farmers against infringement by local officials.

Acknowledgments

I would like to thank Harvey Lam, Jianping Mei, Yan Shen, Xiaobo Zhang and participants of the Conference on Economic Development of Western China, organized by George Tolley at the University of Chicago, and of my lecture in the Contemporary Issues in the Chinese Economy Series sponsored by the Department of Economics and Finance at the City University of Hong Kong for helpful comments; and the Center for Economic Policy Studies and the Gregory C. Chow Econometric Research Program at Princeton University for financial support in the preparation of this paper.

References

Chen, Guidi and Wu Chuntao. *Zhongguo Nongmin Diaocha* [*China Famers Survey*]. Taipei: Dadi (Great Earth) Publishing Company, 2005. (In Chinese.)

Chen, Xiwen. "Conflicts and problems facing china's current rural reform and Development," Chapter 4 in Dong, Song and Zhang, eds. *China's Agricultural Development: Challenges and Prospects*. Hampshire: Ashgate Publishing Limited, 2006.

Chow, Gregory C. *China's Economic Transformation.* Oxford: Blackwell Publishing Company 2002.

Chow, Gregory C. "Corruption and China's economic reform in the early 21st century." *Journal of International Business*, 20 (2006): 263–80.

Dong, Xiao-yuan, Shunfeng Song and Xiaobo Zhang, eds. *China's Agricultural Development: Challenges and Prospects*. Hampshire: Ashgate Publishing Limited, 2006.

Han, Jun. "Jiang tudi nongmin jiti suyou dingjie wei an gufen gongyouzhi" [Chinese collective land ownership into shareholder ownership]. *Zhongguo Ji ngji Shibao* [*China Economic Times*], November 11, 2003. (In Chinese.)

Zeng Yesong. *Xin Nong Lun* [*New Farm Treatise*]. Beijing: Xin Hua Publishing Company, 2004. (In Chinese.)

Zhang Xiabo. "Asymmetric Property Rights in China's Economic Growth." DSGD Discussion Paper No. 28, January 2006. Washington, D. C.: International Food Research Institute, Development Strategy and Government Division.

27

Why is Healthcare in China So Expensive?

There is an old Chinese saying that commodities that are scarce are expensive. This is what the modern economic theory of demand and supply teaches us. When supply is scarce, price is high. When demand increases and supply is fixed or increases little, price will increase. This simple statement answers the question of this essay.

First, let us look at the facts about the increase in price and the slow increase in supply of healthcare services in China. According to *China Statistical Yearbook*, the price index of healthcare services in the years from 1996 to 2006 increased respectively by 12.4, 22.9, 17.2, 11.7, 11.1, 10.5, 8.2, 8.9, 5.2, 5.2 and 3.0 percent. Such a rapid increase in price was remarkable in view of the stability of the consumer price index during these years.

On the slow increase in supply, consider the several measures of supply given in the table below based on *China Statistical Yearbook 2007*, Tables 22-26 and 22-27. Table 1 gives numbers of (1) total employed persons, (2) medical/technical persons, (3) doctors and (4) beds per 10,000 persons in China's health institutions.

Table 1 Employed persons and beds in health institutions (per 10,000 persons).

	Total employed	Medical/Technical	Doctors	Beds
1991	502.5	398.5	15.6	265.5
1992	514.0	407.4	15.7	270.9
1993	521.5	411.7	15.8	276.7
1994	530.7	419.9	16.0	280.3
1995	537.3	425.7	16.2	279.6
1996	541.9	431.2	16.2	283.4
1997	551.6	439.8	16.5	286.9
1998	553.6	442.4	16.5	287.8
1999	557.0	445.9	16.7	289.1
2000	559.1	449.1	16.8	290.8
2001	558.4	450.8	16.9	290.2
2002	523.8	427.0	14.7	290.7
2003	527.5	430.6	14.8	295.5
2004	535.7	439.3	15.0	304.6
2005	542.7	446.0	15.2	313.5
2006	562.0	462.4	15.4	327.1

We can see that the total number of persons employed was about the same in 1996 as in 2004 and that the number of hospital beds increased by only slightly over 10 percent during this period. Note the higher rates of increase of these measures since 2004 that help to explain the slower increase in the price of healthcare during this period as mentioned in the last paragraph.

We now give the reason for the slow increase in the supply of healthcare services and suggest a solution to increase it. The reason is that in China, healthcare provision is the responsibility of the national government and the national government gives this responsibility to local governments. Local governments have limited revenue and most of them prefer to use the limited revenue for economic development while providing just sufficient healthcare to satisfy their responsibility.

A simple solution to the problem of limited supply of healthcare is to allow and encourage supply by people-operated (*minban*) healthcare institutions practicing Western or Chinese medicine. China has long allowed and encouraged *minban* schools to supply education even though the provision of education is also the responsibility of the government. *Minban* healthcare institutions will not only increase supply but provide competition to public health institutions to improve the quality of healthcare services. I cannot think of any other government policy which would be so simple to apply and would have so large an effect to improve the economic wellbeing of the Chinese people. For example, the strategy of the Western Development requires a large amount of capital and the performance of difficult tasks in administering development projects. The change of policy on healthcare would be a simple announcement on the part of the central government.

There are a number of objections to allowing and encouraging people-operated healthcare institutions. First, it is said that the government would lose control of the provision of healthcare. This is not the case since the government will continue to regulate the behavior of *minban* healthcare institutions just as it regulates private industrial and commercial enterprises and *minban* schools. Second, some claim that the provision of healthcare should be treated differently from the provision of other goods or services because doctors know more than patients about what they should want (known as "asymmetric information" between the supplier and the consumer in economics) and therefore can exploit patients by charging them more than required. This is true to some extent but patients cannot be assumed to be entirely ignorant as they can consult with friends and other doctors. More importantly for the present essay, such exploitation by doctors exists as much in public hospitals as in private hospitals.

Third, some consider this policy infeasible because of the resistance of central and local healthcare officials who may have vested interest in protecting public healthcare institutions and argue against the establishment of private hospitals. To solve this political problem, the central government does not need to decide in principle whether *minban* healthcare institutions are more desirable or better than public institutions. It only needs to give the green light for them to come forth. If the *minban* institutions are worse than the public institutions, patients will not go to them. A main reason for the success of China's economic reform was to allow nongovernment institutions to compete with government institutions, such as township and village enterprises and private competing enterprises with state-owned enterprises.

A related objection is that some local governments may be reluctant to encourage *minban* healthcare institutions to operate in its locality. In my proposal the central government need not interfere with local governments' policy regarding healthcare except that the right to establish *minban* healthcare institutions is guaranteed as a national policy. Some local governments may be reluctant to encourage *minban* health institutions or to allow its hospitals to be leased for private operations. They should show discretion in carrying out their policy regarding the extent of encouraging the private operation of healthcare institutions. Incentives to lighten their financial burden and to improve the wellbeing of its people would cause many local governments to adopt this policy, while others will wait and see. The central government can leave the introduction of private healthcare institutions to the discretion of local governments and be confident that if the experiments are successful, more local governments will adopt it.

Before closing, let me stress that this essay deals only with the supply side of healthcare. It discusses who provides it, and not how to pay for it. China has recently introduced different ways to improve health insurance policies, which are not the subject of this essay. One may ask whether insurance money can be used to pay for the cost of using private hospitals and whether local government subsidies should also be provided to private hospitals. My answer to the first question is yes, in order to provide competition. To the second question, my answer is the same as in the last paragraph. It is up to the local governments to decide for their locality. Incentives to increase competition and to improve the wellbeing of its people would lead many local governments to provide equal subsidies to all healthcare institutions. It is even better if the subsidies go to the patients in the form of insurance coverage so that they can decide which hospitals to go to. Hospitals charging high prices and offering poor quality will have to change or they cannot survive.

28

How to Solve the Problem of Income Inequality

A common solution to the problem of income inequality is to tax the rich more and use the proceeds to subsidize the poor. Income tax is known to have economic disadvantages because it taxes people when they try to produce in order to increase their income and thus provides a disincentive to work. A better tax is a tax on consumption which would discourage consumption and thus encourage savings and help promote economic growth.

The proposal that I present today to solve the problem of income inequality is to provide a market that encourages and fosters the voluntary redistribution of income. Many rich people are willing to contribute to improve the welfare of the poor. Charitable contributions are widespread in the US and are gaining popularity in China, especially after the tragic earthquake of May 12. If we can find a way to increase charitable activities, income inequality in China will be reduced.

The main idea is to provide a market that makes it more convenient and efficient for people to contribute. Thus, those people who are willing to contribute will contribute more. Many people would be willing to pay for some projects that are beneficial to the poor if they could find the right opportunity. They want to make sure that the contributions are spent for a good cause and will not be wasted. The recipient has to be trustworthy and effective in using the contribution for a cause that the contributor deems worthwhile. To achieve this, we need an information network. I believe that a major newspaper can provide such a network. It can set up a clearinghouse-type website for potential beneficiaries and contributors to communicate. The website can list all potential beneficiaries according to the location and nature of the project. The location specifies the province, city, county or even village. The nature of the charitable work may be to support schools, hospitals, etc. and may include other specifications. Any institution, be it a local government unit or a potential head of an institution, can submit a proposal outlining its nature and purpose and the cost involved. A potential contributor has the option to list the nature of projects that he will be interested in supporting. The format for the proposals and the details for this information network have to be carefully worked out by the newspaper willing to provide this information network.

All potential donors can search for projects which they are interested in supporting and explore options further with the institutions. On reaching an agreement, the two parties will proceed according to the way they choose and work out the details by themselves. The sponsoring newspaper will receive a statement that a contract has been reached and a summary of the terms of contract (details of the contract to be specified by the newspaper). It will be up to the newspaper to decide whether to charge a fee when the contract is signed. It seems reasonable to charge a fee. The fee may be collected from the institution or donor at the time the information is submitted to the newspaper for inclusion in the network. It may also include a small percentage of the total contributions for the first year (or two) of operation after an agreement is reached, up to a specified maximum amount. Imposing a fee that is too large would encourage parties to avoid payment – they can always claim that they have found each other through other sources of information, especially for donors who do not register with the network.

Besides serving as an information network, the sponsoring newspaper can serve as an enforcer of the contract defining the terms of the contribution. If the recipient turns out to be dishonest or incompetent, he may be exposed. The fear of exposure by the media serves to enforce honesty and good work. In addition, examples of outstanding success will have a chance of being publicized so that the contributor to and the manager and staff of the project such as a school or a hospital will receive due credit. Furthermore, serving as an enforcer enables the newspaper to collect its fee when the contract is signed.

To use income tax to equalize the distribution of income has its economic disadvantages, as I have pointed out in the introduction. Besides providing disincentives for people to work hard to increase their income, an income tax system run by the government has many drawbacks. The administrative cost of collecting the tax for the government is very large, and the cost borne by the taxpayers to manipulate tax returns and to find ways to avoid taxes, including the cost of the taxpayer's time in keeping all tax-related records and the cost of lawyers and tax accountants, are even larger. (Many countries in the world have an income tax system that provides revenue for the government to do many useful things, besides the redistribution of income. The purpose of this article is to find a way to improve the redistribution of income without interfering with the existing tax system.) The proposed way of redistributing income is voluntary. It involves no coercion. It improves the economic welfare of all concerned, not only the recipient organizations and the beneficiaries but also the donors, simply by allowing them the opportunity to do what they desire (without hurting others).

Finally, such activities will improve the building of a harmonious society in China. The satisfaction of being able to help others and seeing the fruits of your effort, or of receiving help from others when you need it, can help promote the moral values of the society besides bridging the gap between the rich and the poor from an economic point of view.

29

Can We Understand Corruption Using Tools of Economics?

It has been observed that corruption has increased in China. This is my observation as well. Given that this is true, let me try to explain it using the basic tools of economics. Given an understanding of this phenomenon, perhaps we can suggest ways to reduce it.

Let me begin with a definition of corruption. It is the illegal use of public or government assets for private gains where assets include the power to grant material or other benefits. By this definition, corruption cannot occur without the control of government assets.

To understand the reason for an increase in corruption, we can appeal to the economic forces of demand and supply. Corruption has increased because the demand for it has increased and the supply of it has also increased in the last 20 years.

Demand has increased because during the period of economic prosperity after economic reform, there has been an increase in the need to obtain government approval to carry out many economic activities. To establish and operate a business enterprise, to export and import, to introduce a new product, to obtain a bank loan and to obtain the right to use a piece of land all require approval of government officials. On the side of supply, the number of government officials appointed to perform such services and the spheres of their power have also increased to satisfy the needs of the market. As a result of the increases in both the demand for and the supply of such illegal activities, corruption has increased.

There is a kind of minor corruption which is socially acceptable. In such cases the government official does perform a service when approving an activity of a customer, such as checking whether his exports or imports satisfy the legal requirement or whether the new drug introduced passes certain standards, but collects a fee which is illegal because he works for the government. One example is the fee charged by an official of a bank in extending a loan to a borrower. It this is a private bank which pays the loan official according to the amount of loans extended, the payment for the service is perfectly legal. A second example is the fee a doctor in private practice charges his patient for services rendered, which is certainly proper and legal. On the other hand, if the banker works in a government bank which pays him a fixed monthly salary or if the doctor works in a public hospital paying him a fixed salary regardless of the amount of services performed, it would be illegal and considered corruption for him to receive compensation according to the service performed. In the Chinese society it is socially acceptable if a government official receives a moderate amount of compensation for services rendered.

It is socially unacceptable and harmful to the social and political stability if government officials receive large sums of money through corruption. The corruption may be the embezzlement of public assets and bribery from citizens. Bank officials have embezzled large amounts of funds to personal accounts. Officials with the power to approve new drugs have received very large amounts of money from drug producers. The Chinese government has taken such cases of corruption seriously and has tried to punish the offenders, including sentencing them to death, but the practice has continued.

Given that the basic cause of corruption is the need for the services performed by government officials, one way to reduce corruption would be to reduce the areas requiring government approval in the conduct of economic activities mentioned above. Even in the case of the approval of new drugs being introduced into the market, it may be desirable to reduce the degree to which government approval is required. Consumers would take more risk in choosing the drugs they need with the advice of their physicians but they would have more drugs from which to choose. Traditional China did not have government officials to approve any of the herbal medicine freely brought and sold and the extent of abuse was under control. Readers might disagree on the extent that the government should regulate this particular activity but most would agree that transferring public enterprises to private ownerships would make enterprise officials collecting fees for service a legal activity. Furthermore, allowing public officials to approve the use of land under the system of public ownership of land in China has led to much corruption and serious discontent from farmers in China. Only basic political reform of the use of land would solve this problem

30

How to Improve the Regulation of Industrial Pollution in China

Unlike other useful resources or assets, natural resources have been used freely without being paid for. This leads to abuse and waste by the users. This paper deals with industrial pollution since pollution by consumers is more difficult to track down and requires other tools such as imposing a tax on all users of coal. Economists believing in the market economy recognize that in this area the government has a responsibility to limit the amount of pollution to the environment. How can it achieve this? One standard way is to prohibit air and water pollution by command. Any pollution over a given amount will be prohibited and the polluter punished. There is a second way to limit pollution which has certain advantages over the use of command. It is the use of emission permits. The government issues a certain number of emission permits in a certain area. All industrial polluters are required to purchase permits proportional to the amount of pollution they generate. The government agency responsible receives revenue by selling the permits. If a factory has purchased more permits than it requires because it pollutes less than expected, it can sell the permits to any bidder at market price.

The market of emission permits works in the following way. First, a government environmental protection agency decides on the total number of permits to issue. Given the supply of permits thus determined, the demand by industrial polluters will determine the price of the permits. This is a simple application of the law of supply and demand in economics. Usually the supply curve is positively sloping, showing that when the price increases the suppliers will supply more. The demand curve is negatively sloping, indicating that when the price increases people will buy less. The familiar diagram of a supply curve and a demand curve shows how the price and quantity are determined at the intersection point of the supply and demand curves. In the case of emission permits, the supply curve is vertical if a government agency determines a fixed number of permits to issue. The demand curve will still be negatively sloping because when the price of permits increases, the users of the permits will try to use cleaner energy and save on the number of permits.

The advantage of using permits rather than simply forbidding the polluters to pollute above a certain amount is to provide economic incentive to pollute less by using cleaner energy although clean energy may be more expensive. If polluters are not allowed by command to pollute more than a certain amount, those using clean energy receive no benefits as compared with those polluting up to the limit allowed. Rewarding the use of clean energy will encourage innovations of methods to produce it. The revenue received by the government can also be used to promote the innovation of clean energy. The use of emission permits has been adopted by the European Union to control the amount of carbon dioxide emitted by electricity producers. It has also been used in the United States.

There may be occasions for the use of emission permits in China although there may be cases where regulation by command might be more suitable. Let me propose the following possible institutional arrangement for the use of emission permits consisting of four components:

1. In the case of air or water pollution, the local office of the Ministry of Environmental Protection issues a fixed number of emission permits per period. Each polluter is required to report the amount of pollution during the period and to pay for a number of permits equal to the amount of pollution reported. Self-reporting makes polluters aware of their action and saves the cost of monitoring, provided that false reporting will result in a severe penalty when discovered. The areas to be demarcated for the issue of permits have to be broad enough to cover most of the spillover effect of air and water pollution.

2. Given the number of permits issued, demand by polluters will determine the price of a permit. The Ministry's local office will first set an initial price for the permits. If the price is too low, the permits will run out and some polluters will need to purchase them from others. If the initial price is too high, there will be unsold permits and the local office will lower the price until all permits are sold.

3. In determining the number of permits to issue, the local office of the Ministry takes into account the costs and benefits of pollution and solicits opinions from the directly elected village heads in rural areas and the directly elected representatives in urban areas. Citizens of the area should be consulted through their representatives because they suffer the effects of pollution.

4. The revenue received from the permits will be used to develop clean energy or returned to the local government of the area affected, to be used for the benefit of the citizens as determined by their representatives. Under the proposal, the local residents through their representatives and the local government will have an incentive not only to help determine a suitable amount of pollution permitted but also to help enforce the regulation to limit pollution.

Thus, this proposal will help solve the problem of enforcing environmental regulations. The consumers will try to deter violators in order to protect their environment and protect their revenue from pollution if they receive part of the revenue. In China, both industrial polluters and local government officials who are more concerned with rapid economic growth in their locality than with protecting the environment have contributed to the violation of environmental protection laws. Under this proposal local citizens, in cooperation with officials of the Environmental Protection Ministry, would help enforce environmental protection regulations. The violation of environmental protection laws has resulted in protests by Chinese citizens. This proposal will channel the energy of the protesting citizens to positive action through the government. It also echoes two major directions of China's economic and political development. From the economic point of view, it can be considered a part of the continued reform towards a market economy in harnessing market incentives for the protection of the environment and the use and innovation of clean energy. From the political point of view it is a means of promoting the development of a democratic government by giving power to the people to help make government decisions on the regulation of industrial pollution.

31

China's Successful Experiences in Solving Energy and Environmental Problems

China has been facing serious energy and environmental problems. In the 11th Five-Year Plan a target was to reduce energy consumption for every 10,000 yuan of GDP by 20 percent by 2010, or by 4 percentage points per year. But in 2006 only 1.4 percentage points were achieved. The World Health Organization reports that in 1998, of the ten most polluted cities in the world, seven were in China. It is therefore encouraging to relate two successful experiences in China's effort to solve its energy and environmental problems. In the development of clean energy it has increased the production and export of solar panels significantly. In the control of air pollution it has reduced the emission of SO_2 from power plants by the use of scrubbers.

According to the *New York Times*, August 25, 2009, although solar energy remains far more expensive to generate than energy from coal, oil, natural gas or even wind, the global economic downturn and a decline in European subsidies to buy panels have lowered prices. Chinese companies have played a leading role in reducing the price of solar panels by almost half over the last year. Production of solar panels have increased because production cost in China is lower than in other countries and, since March 2009, the Chinese central and local governments have provided heavy subsidies to solar panel manufacturers, including free land, and cash for research and development. State-owned banks are flooding the industry with loans at considerably lower interest rates than available in Europe or the United States.

The largest company, Suntech in Wuxi, has become the second largest manufacturer in the world, second only to First Solar of the United States. Many firms in China have entered the market. Some are planning to produce in the US to avoid American protectionist policies against imports from China. Although the production of solar power is increasing, it remains a very small source of energy, with an expected total capacity in 2020 (20,000 megawatts) equal to only half of the output of coal power plants built in one year.

The successful development of solar panels shows that the Chinese government is capable of identifying an important product to subsidize in order to promote its production for the purpose of economic development and that the Chinese entrepreneurs are ready to take advantage of the government subsidies and the favorable production and marketing conditions in China to expand the production and export of this product. The government's success in promoting the production of clean energy is not limited to solar panels. China has doubled its total wind energy capacity in each of the past four years, and is poised to pass the United States this year as the world's largest market for wind power equipment. China is also building considerably more nuclear power plants than the rest of the world combined, and these do not emit carbon dioxide after they are built. This article does not discuss whether the cost to the government in promoting clean energy is worth the benefits in each case.

The success story of the control of air pollution by the use of SO_2 scrubbers is reported in a PhD thesis by Xu Yuan (徐袁) at the Woodrow Wilson School of Public and International Affairs at Princeton University. In the 10th Five-Year Plan (2001–2005), China's SO_2 emissions went up by 28 percent and missed the goal of reducing emissions by 10 percent. However, in the 11th Five-Year Plan (2006–2010), the trend was reversed. In 2008, China achieved a 9 percent reduction of SO_2 emissions from the 2005 level, almost reaching the goal of 10 percent by 2010. The most dramatic change happened at coal power plants: China managed to install SO_2 scrubbers at both newly built coal power plants and old ones as retrofits. At the end of 2008, China had 363 GW_e of SO_2 scrubbers, or 60 percent of the total capacity of coal power generation (601 GW_e). By comparison, the ratio at the end of 2005 was only 10 percent.

The achievement came from the central government's effort in mobilizing both the leaders of local governments and managers of coal power plants. For the former, two measures were taken in the 11th Five-Year Plan: 1) promotion and removal of leaders according to the success in the operation of SO_2 scrubbers and 2) using the power to suspend construction of large projects which may affect the environment (including new coal power plants over 200 MW_e) since, by law, large construction projects require ratification by the Ministry of Environmental Protection according to its assessment of the environmental impact of the project. To increase the capacity of supervision by site visits, the total personnel at all government levels increased from 37,934 in 2001 to 52,845 in 2006, or by 39.3 percent.

In providing incentives to managers of power plants, the most important policy in the 11th Five-Year Plan for the operation of SO_2 scrubbers is called "desulfurized electricity price premium." After installing an SO_2 scrubber, a coal power plant is allowed to sell its electricity to the electric grid at a price 15 RMB/MWh higher than the original price, if the SO_2 scrubber is under normal operation; it would be fined 75 RMB/MWh if its SO_2 scrubber were shut down. Although many coal power plants with SO_2 scrubbers were receiving the price premium as early as 2004, the penalty and other detailed regulations were not enforced until July 2007.

What are the reasons for the success in the control of SO_2 emissions? Will the same factors work for controlling air pollution in China in general? There are two conditions favorable to the success in the use of SO_2 scrubbers. First, the source of pollution, namely coal power plants, is easy to identify and control. Second, the method of solution by the use of scrubbers is clear-cut. Hence it is easy to design policies for the local government officials and plant managers to follow. Other cases of air pollution by consumers and by other industrial producers may be more difficult to identify and the methods of solution may not be as straightforward. However, the success in the case of SO_2 scrubbers has demonstrated the resolve and the ability of the central government in controlling air pollution. Given its resolve, we can expect that the government will try to deal with the more difficult cases even if the effort may be less successful and more time-consuming. The government has also learned from this successful experience.

In promoting economic development, the Chinese government fosters the production of new products and prevents economic production from harming the environment. It is encouraging to record a successful example in each of these two undertakings

32

A Proposal to Regulate CO_2 Emissions Through the United Nations

Al Gore, former Vice President and presidential candidate of the Democratic Party, received a Nobel Peace Prize last year for his contribution to regulate the emission of CO_2 in order to prevent harmful climate change. The scientific community agrees that if the amount of CO_2 in the atmosphere becomes twice the amount that existed before the Industrial Revolution, an intolerable level of global warming will occur. If the rate of carbon emissions increases at the rate it did in the last 30 years, this dangerous level will be reached in about 70 years. Therefore, to slow down the emission of CO_2 is a most urgent task. The task is difficult because people are accustomed to using coal at home for cooking and heating and in factories to generate electricity, and to using oil for heating and fueling automobiles. All such uses of fossil fuels to generate energy cause the emission of carbon dioxide.

Scientists and scholars have proposed different rates for reducing CO_2 emissions and different schemes for nations to share the reduction. Any proposal by a scientist or scholar to limit carbon emissions is irrelevant unless nations can agree on it. Rather than adding to this list of recommendations, I would

like to propose a way for the nations to reach an agreement on what they wish to do. My proposal is through a reasonable and democratic process by which nations can reach a solution of their own, rather than proposing a solution of my own that they should adopt.

The proposal is based on the following propositions which I hope most citizens and nations in the world can accept.

1. CO_2 emissions are affecting the atmosphere, which is a valuable resource.
2. The atmosphere is collectively owned by the citizens of the world as presented by their national governments, with equal right of ownership to all citizens.
3. Any amount of CO_2 emissions in any country has to be paid for by obtaining emission permits.

Based on these propositions, the following resolution can be proposed to the United Nations. The resolution consists of the following components:

1. Each member of the United Nations submits a desired amount of total world emissions of CO_2 for a given period (of one to three years). The median amount will be adopted.
2. Emission permits are required when carbon is emitted. The total number of permission permits or the total amount of world emissions should be distributed equally to the world's citizens under the assumption that each person has an equal right to use the atmosphere in the form of carbon emissions.
3. Emission permits, once distributed to the nations, can be bought and sold at prices mutually agreed upon.

4. The government of each country has the responsibility to insure that the total amount of emissions in the country shall not exceed the amount allowed by the permits that it possesses.

To carry out this resolution, nations are required only to vote on the total amount of emissions allowed and ensure the amount emitted in their own territory equals the number of permits they possess.

The above proposal can be interpreted as a version of "cap and trade" for CO_2 emission permits, except that it includes specific procedures to determine the total amount of emissions allowed in the world and the distribution of this amount to all nations.

Less developed countries like China and India are likely to support this proposal because their current emissions per capita is below the world average and they will benefit from selling their permits to other countries.

However, some developed countries like the United States may not be willing to limit its per capita emissions to the world average. Under this proposal it needs to purchase permits from the world market, which it can afford. The proposal only stipulates that US citizens are entitled to the same number of emission permits or to the use of the same amount of the world atmosphere as other world citizens. If they use more, they need to pay for it. In so doing they are subsidizing the less developed countries in the protection of the environment as many have proclaimed they are willing to do. This resolution may not be popular in the United States, but the citizens of the US should understand that citizens of other countries have an equal right to use the atmosphere and that if they wish to use more per person they should pay for it by purchasing emission permits in the world market. This proposal would not only help to protect the world environment but would give the United States an opportunity to regain its moral leadership if it chooses to embrace it.

Part 4

Thoughts About the American Economy

33

Milton Friedman — as a Scholar, as a Person — and China

On November 15, 2006, as I was traveling from Princeton to New York, I heard on the radio that Milton Friedman had passed away earlier that morning. The news was extremely sad indeed!

Once a leader of the Chicago School of Economics, Milton Friedman was the most influential economist in the second half of the 20th century. John Maynard Keynes was the most influential in the first. Observing the Great Depression in the early 1930s, Keynes questioned the proper functioning of the market economy. On the other hand, Friedman had faith in the market economy. Keynes thought that when aggregate output increased in a market economy, consumption would fail to catch up, leading to insufficient aggregate demand and thus requiring the intervention of the government to increase its expenditures to make up the insufficient demand. Friedman disagreed with this viewpoint and believed that the ratio of aggregate consumption to aggregate output or income is constant as the economy grows, provided that income is measured by "permanent income" which in turn is measured by the long-run purchasing power of the consumers. In 1957 he published this view in his book *A Theory of the Consumption Function* for which he was awarded the Nobel Prize in 1976.

Friedman made another important contribution to economics. He argued that the Great Depression of the 1930s was due to mistakes in the government's monetary policy. This viewpoint was seriously debated in the 1950s but his view on monetary policy finally prevailed. He advocated that the monetary authority should maintain a constant rate of increase in the supply of money because such a policy would reduce macroeconomic fluctuations and help maintain a stable price level. This policy recommendation has had a great impact on the conduct of monetary policies by the Federal Reserve System in the US and by the central banks of other countries since.

Friedman's mind was very sharp. He responded swiftly in debates. He commanded great respect as a scholar. When I entered the University of Chicago to pursue graduate work in economics, I heard about his great reputation. He was revered by students in his first-year class on price theory. In my four years at Chicago I discovered his intellectual power, high standard in scholarship and swift reaction in intellectual debate. Once I presented part of my dissertation in his workshop on money. He was extremely critical, challenging every major point I made but after the workshop session he told me, "I would not have challenged your presentation so much if your work had not been a good piece of research." This gave me much encouragement. I received a job offer to teach at MIT after receiving my PhD on account of his letter of recommendation.

Friedman and I maintained a friendship after I left Chicago and until his passing. He endorsed my 2004 book *Knowing China*. In 1988 he visited China and met with Premier Zhao Ziyang. He was much impressed by Zhao's understanding of economics. After visiting China and Hong Kong several times, he was impressed by the economic growth of China and the free market economy of Hong Kong.

Of all my teachers, Friedman has had the most influence on me in how to do research in economics and how to help improve society. In doing research, Friedman chose only important and relevant problems to study. He was not interested in abstract theory which has no relevance to the real world. He was able to see the crux of a problem rather than getting tied down by details. He believed that a simple theory with a few variables is better than a complicated theory with many variables if the former can explain the phenomenon equally well. To him, a good economist should look for simple theories that are applicable to different countries and different times as much as possible. His permanent income hypothesis and his monetary theory are some examples. I give another example below.

Ben Bernanke, the current chairman of the Board of Governors of the Federal System in the US is a great admirer of Friedman's. At a conference in Texas about three years ago, Bernanke presented a paper showing that a Friedman proposition concerning the effects of an exogenous change in money supply on output and prices is valid for many time periods and countries. The proposition states that the effect on output will occur soon but be short-lived while the effect on prices will be delayed but long-lasting. I decided to test this proposition for China. When I started my research Friedman told me that his proposition would be valid for China. He was right!

In trying to help improve the society, Friedman did not believe in taking high government positions. Through his writing and his influence on his students, he had a greater effect on the economies of the world than almost any government official that I can think of. His books and his students have had an important influence on the economic development of China.

Friedman had opinions about China which turned out to be incorrect but he was willing to admit his mistakes. Soon after the tragic incident in Tiananmen Square on June 4, 1989, Friedman wrote an article in *San Francisco Chronicle* predicting economic catastrophe, including runaway inflation in China.

A couple of years later or so, when I received a book of his writings from him which included this article, I emailed him to point out that his pessimistic forecast for 1989 was somewhat off the mark. He replied, "What do you mean somewhat off the mark? It was a huge mistake! This teaches me not to predict events in China, a country about which I do not know." When Hong Kong was to be returned to China in 1997 under the principle of "one country, two systems" including a separate currency for Hong Kong, Friedman told me that having two currencies in one country would be impossible. He turned out to be wrong again!

Later on, Friedman's view of China became more positive and optimistic. In an interview published by the *Wall Street Journal* in June 2004, he predicted that within 75 years, China's economy would become the largest in the world.

34

How are American Universities Different from the Chinese?

The best universities in the United States are also recognized as the best in the world. This statement was not true before World War II. At that time many universities in Europe were better than the best in the US. Since World War II many distinguished scholars have migrated to the United States. Since the end of the war, peace, economic prosperity and an attractive academic environment have attracted more distinguished scholars to the US and produced scholars in the US. This is the first difference.

Second, given the fact that American universities are now at the top, it is difficult for other countries to catch up in one or two decades. A main reason is that the accumulation of human capital is a slow process. Just the training of one qualified professor requires some 20 years after obtaining high school education. Having a group of top scholars working together in one university is much more difficult to establish because the top scholars are mostly satisfied with their working environment and are not willing to move to another institution unless it has other equally able colleagues. In recent years China's universities have been able to improve rapidly because the economic conditions have improved and many universities are able to attract groups of young PhD holders to return to China, as well as smaller numbers of established overseas Chinese scholars, to return to China by providing very good working conditions.

Third, the promotion of faculty members in the US is by and large based on a set of objective criteria. Promotion at each level from assistant professorship to associate and to full professorship requires the approval of colleagues at higher levels and of a university-wide committee which also solicits written evaluation from scholars outside the university. The main criterion is scholarship, i.e., having made important contributions to the field. Professors of all ranks can advise PhD students in their thesis while in China only professors with the title of PhD adviser can perform such a function.

In China, a professor is said to "lead" a PhD student where in the US there is less of a hierarchical distinction. Professors consider advising PhD students a mutually learning process. An indication of the difference in attitude is that when a PhD student is close to finishing his degree he often is asked to address his adviser and other professors by their first name. This is unheard of in China. Some professors close to retirement age still refer to their former professors as Professor or Teacher in China.

Most top departments in the US do not keep their own PhD students as junior faculty members in order to get new ideas from young scholars trained elsewhere. In China many PhD holders stay in their own schools and follow the research work of their own teachers.

Fourth, in accepting graduate students the American system is more objective. The decision to offer acceptance to a student for graduate study is made by a committee, with rotating membership, on the basis of his ability to pursue graduate work. The academic performance is based partly on tests given by the Education Testing Service administered nationally. In China, a professor with the rank of PhD adviser can select students to study under his supervision. The training in the US is also more objective, requiring the ability to pass examinations in specific fields and to complete an original piece of research as judged by a committee of faculty members, plus defending the thesis in an oral examination open to all members of the faculty. In China, a graduate student studies under the guidance of one professor and his research requires the approval of this professor only. In recent years, the Chinese system has been changing, with some universities following some of the practices of the American system.

In the acceptance of undergraduate students, the American system often considers non-academic qualifications including leadership quality, skills in sports and music, and personal interest and initiative. In China, performance in a purely academic examination administered nationally is the only criterion for acceptance by universities.

Fifth, a large number of top US universities are private whereas all top universities in china are public and under the supervision of the Ministry of Education. Before 1952, China also had very good private universities but they were absorbed by public universities in 1952 when the higher education system was modeled after the system of the Soviet Union. Universities were divided according to broad fields of study in order to offer specialized training to students serving in specific fields in a planned economy. Such specialized universities have been combined to form larger and more comprehensive universities after economic reform started in 1978.

Sixth, American universities are independent whereas Chinese universities are subject to the control of the government. The top national universities are under the control of the Ministry of Education. The Ministry has the power to decide on the number of MBA students that a university can accept and to approve the plan of a professor wishing to travel abroad to do research or to visit a foreign university.

Seventh, college students in the US have more freedom to select the courses they wish to take and have a much smaller number of required courses. In addition, Chinese students have to declare their major before starting as a freshman while most American students declare their major at the end of their sophomore year. Students in the US majoring in one subject are allowed to select more courses in other fields to broaden their education.

Eighth, the quality of American universities widely varies whereas in China the Ministry of Education enforces a certain set of standards for all universities. America has more universities for the size of its population. Most high school graduates can enter some university or college.

Ninth, to improve the student's personal behavior and to educate him on his civic duties are not responsibilities of an American university. The traditional education in China includes moral behavior, academic knowledge, health and social responsibilities or skills as the four major components. This carries over to some extent to university education today.

Tenth, many top American universities have a large endowment from which a sizable part, up to a third, of total expenditures are drawn. The Woodrow Wilson School of Public and International Affairs at Princeton University alone recently had an endowment of its own of over 800 million dollars. It pays all the tuition and living expenses for all students studying towards a master's degree in public administration. The Chinese national universities depend mainly on allocation from the Ministry of Education and collection of tuition from students to pay their expenses.

Eleventh, students in American universities have a variety of activities besides academic study. These include sports, music appreciation and performance, theatre, arts and social activities of student groups. These help them to become well-rounded persons. These serve as substitutes for the education on morals, knowledge acquisition, health and social skills directed by elders in China.

Finally, it has been observed that the American college education emphasizes the development of independent and critical thinking. Chinese college students mainly receive the transfer of knowledge from their professors. To the extent that this is true, some graduate students having graduated from China and studying in American universities may excel in passing examinations but find it more difficult to do an original piece of research for their PhD thesis, but many Chinese students excel in both, showing that one can still learn at the stage of graduate school even if the undergraduate education is somewhat inferior.

35

What You Need to Know to Apply to Elite American Universities

You or your children may be thinking of applying to elite American universities. What are these universities like? What are your chances of getting in? What are the criteria by which they accept applicants? I have taught at elite American universities including MIT, Cornell, Harvard, Columbia and Princeton since obtaining my PhD degree from the University of Chicago in 1955 and should be able to say something on these questions. I am now further informed by a recent book, *No Longer Separate, Not Yet Equal: Race and Class in Elite College Admission and Campus Life* (Princeton University Press, 2009), written by two colleagues Thomas Espenshade and Alexandria Walton Radford, and can provide better answers to the above questions. The title of this new book reflects a phrase in the history of American education, "separate but equal." This phrase refers to schools provided to black and white Americans at the time. The authors point out that while the schools are no longer separate, they are not yet equal for black and white students applying to and studying in elite universities.

Let me start with the fact that there is a growing Chinese presence on American college campuses. According to the newly released 2009 *Open Doors* report, the number of Chinese (graduate and undergraduate) students enrolled in US colleges and universities jumped by more than 21 percent between the fall of 2007 and fall of 2008. Undergraduate enrollment from China rose by an eye-popping 60 percent. Last academic year, China accounted for 98,200 international students in the US, or nearly 15 percent of the total, just behind India with 103,300. China could move ahead of India this year.

These patterns are most evident at the selective colleges and universities – those that admit a very small fraction of applicants. At Princeton University, for example, where just 10 percent of applicants were admitted to the graduating class of 2013, the share of Asian students (including Asian-American and international students) among entering first-year students has been rising steadily. In the fall of 2004, only 12.1 percent of all first-year students were classified as Asian. This proportion grew to 17.7 percent by the fall of 2009. Partly because the size of the entering class also increased, the number of Asian first-year (undergraduate) students at Princeton has shot up by 60 percent in the past five years.

It is important to know that admission to an elite college is not based on the score on a single test. Academic excellence, as measured by course grades and test scores, surely counts. But so does being a black or Hispanic student, a star athlete, the child of a former graduate, and attending an outstanding secondary school. A minority student is favored because of the "affirmative action" adopted by President Kennedy in 1961 as a method of redressing racial discrimination. Having parents who can pay the full college fee – which now tops $50,000 a year at the best private institutions – also matters. At Princeton, however, a policy to admit freshmen without regard to the financial need of applicants was introduced in 2004. This policy was followed by other Ivy League universities including Harvard and Yale. Princeton has an endowment of about

17 billion dollars and is therefore rich enough to adopt such a policy. Having accepted the students it wants, Princeton will provide financial support to those who need it, with the amount dependent on the financial condition of the student's family.

In an elite college, Chinese students could face an "Asian penalty." Other things equal, Asian students need SAT scores 140 points higher than whites and 450 points higher than blacks (on the old 1600-point scale) to have the same chance of being admitted to a selective private university. This disadvantage is smaller for first-generation and international Asian students than for Asian-Americans who are born in the United States and have a foreign-born parent.

Classes at selective American colleges involve lectures and small-group discussions. Students debate each other, and it is not a sign of disrespect to disagree with a professor. Graduation rates are high at the selective schools that Espenshade and Radford study. Rates of graduation within six years reach 89 percent overall, and jump to 92 percent for Asians. Asian students are overrepresented in the natural sciences and engineering, but are underrepresented in the humanities. Academically, they perform almost as well as their white counterparts, and substantially better than their black or Hispanic peers.

Elite American colleges value "diversity" and encourage undergraduates from different racial groups to mingle on campus. While white students are the most racially isolated group, Asian students are slightly more likely to interact with non-Asian students than they are with other Asians. In general, patterns of social interaction across racial and ethnic lines exhibit a "racial hierarchy" that reflects each group's economic and social position in contemporary American society. "Racial hierarchy" is what members of the society perceive. Whites are at the top, blacks are at the bottom, and Asians and Hispanics are in between in that order.

Two-thirds of students who attend selective American colleges are highly satisfied with their overall academic experiences; this proportion applies also to Asian students. Note that in the US there are many private universities and most of the very top universities are private, unlike China where all top universities are public. In general, students at private colleges are happier with their academic experiences than are students at public universities. Nearly 60 percent of these students are highly satisfied with their social experiences, a proportion that also characterizes Asian students.

The names of Princeton, Harvard and Yale are known the world over. Enrolling at one of these – or another highly selective college or university – confers status. But it also means that one is more likely to graduate, more likely to enroll subsequently in a graduate or professional school, and more likely to have a higher lifetime income. No wonder, then, that Harvard accepted just 7.1 percent of all applicants for undergraduate admission in the fall of 2008, and Yale admitted only 9.3 percent. If you have been accepted, my sincere congratulations. If you or your children are applying, may I wish you success.

36

The Financial Crisis and the World Economy

The current financial crisis originated in the United States and has spread to other major countries in the world. To understand the global financial crisis we first explain what it is and how it came about in the United States.

In a financial crisis, banks and other financial institutions have bad assets and do not have sufficient funds to lend to businesses to meet their payrolls and to order goods for sale or to lend to consumers to finance their purchases of automobiles. Some major banks in the US went out of business. This lack of liquidity prevented businesses from functioning and put people out of work.

In the United States the crisis was caused by a housing bubble; this means that the prices of houses went up a lot and then fell rapidly. As housing prices increased, consumers were encouraged to buy larger houses and take larger mortgages that charged interest rates that can change in the future. When housing prices came down and the interest rate went up, home owners could not pay the interest on their mortgages. The mortgages became bad assets of the financial institutions holding them. Banks which owned the mortgages directly or owned securities backed by the mortgages went bankrupt. Owners had their houses foreclosed and lost their homes. Some people hold the government responsible for reducing the regulation of commercial banks and allowing them to hold risky assets (including risky securities backed by mortgages and the mortgages themselves). Some blame the financial institutions and realtors for overselling their products to consumers. Some say that the house buyers are also to blame since they bought a large house or took a larger mortgage for an existing house to spend the money on other consumer goods which they could not afford when bad times came.

To prevent further collapse of financial institutions, the US Congress adopted on Friday, October 3, 2008, a rescue plan proposed by Treasury Secretary Paulson. The plan is to buy bad assets from financial institutions to the amount of $700 billion. The bill passed after a short deliberation of less than ten days because members of Congress did not want to be held responsible for letting the economy go down, although they received objections from many voters that the plan would amount to using taxpayers' money to bail out rich financial institutions which took risky investments and should be responsible for subsequent losses.

The Treasury will purchase bad assets from financial institutions up to $700 billion in stages, with $250 billion available immediately. In addition, the bill temporarily raises the amount of bank deposits insured by the government from $100,000 to $250,000. It calls on federal agencies to encourage loan servicers to modify existing mortgages by reducing the principal or interest rate. The amount of debt forgiven by a bank to a borrower in a foreclosure can be deducted from federal income tax. Federal Reserve Chairman Ben Bernanke said of the bill, "The legislation is a critical step toward stabilizing our financial markets and ensuring an uninterrupted flow of credit to households and businesses."

Economists have raised the following objections to the rescue plan:

1. If the government is known to bail out failing businesses, in the future businesses will take risks and count on the government to bail them out.
2. The plan amounts to giving too much power to the government in interfering with the functions of the US market economy by purchasing a huge amount of financial assets directly, as never before done in US history.
3. The plan was adopted too hastily without giving sufficient time for deliberation and to get opinions from experts.
4. Without the plan, the market itself will adjust, even after some painful economic experience. The prices of houses will go up when it has gone down far enough. People will start buying homes and the bad mortgages will reduce in number.
5. Even if one agrees to the plan in principle, it is very difficult to implement in practice. Who will decide and what criteria are used to decide which financial assets to buy among so many available in the US? At what prices should the assets be purchased? Paulson has a difficult task in organizing a team of many people to select which financial assets to buy. The financial institutions not being bailed out will complain of unfair treatment.
6. The government may purchase the banks' bad assets but the banks may still hold on to much of their money and will not lend it out. Only when the banks are confident that the borrowers will repay the loans, will they decide to extend the loans. Since the economy is in a serious regression, many businesses are in trouble and many cannot convince the banks to lend money to them. This in turns slows down economic recovery.

Whether the bailout bill is good cannot be decided even two years from now or after the recovery of the economy. First, it may be unfair if some prudent people are hurt by having to pay more taxes to finance the rescue package while others involved in risky investment or having purchased houses which they could not afford will gain. Second, future events cannot reveal whether the bailout plan has helped. Whatever the degree of recovery, we do not know what would have happened without the bailout. Third, the result will depend on how well the bailout plan is carried out. If the Treasury buys the assets at low prices, the government holding the assets or the taxpayers will gain; if at high prices, the bailout will be more costly, and the loss to taxpayers may outweigh the gain in helping the market or the economy recover sooner.

In addition to the above rescue plan, the Federal Reserve took action in early October to change its policy by buying commercial papers from (unsecured short-term loans to) businesses directly (rather than indirectly by providing banks with more funds to lend out to businesses). On October 8, the Fed lowered the federal fund rate (used by commercial banks to borrow money) by half of a percentage point to 1.5 percent. The latter action was taken simultaneously by six other central banks of major countries, including China.

In early October major countries in Europe were facing a similar financial crisis.

Major banks in the United Kingdom, Germany and France went bankrupt or were taken over by the government. The stock prices in European and Asian stock markets also went down rapidly, just as in the United States where stock prices (Standard & Poor's 500 stocks) on October 9 went down by over 40 percent from the high point a year before. The crisis is global and many economies are in recession. The US financial crisis spread to other countries because they own bad financial assets of the United States.

When will the crisis be over and when will the major economies be rid of their recessions? No one can predict because short-term economic fluctuations are very difficult to predict. The speed of recovery depends on the psychology of all actors in the economy. If the bankers believe the economy will soon turn better, they will be more willing to lend to businesses. The businesses will in turn expand their output and possibly hire more people. Given the prospect of employment opportunities, people will spend more, leading to more output of consumer goods, and so forth. In each step the outcome depends on what people think.

While many other countries are experiencing financial crisis, China's financial institutions remain relatively sound because the Chinese banks are more strictly regulated and could not take risky investments as banks in the US did. Even if Chinese banks have bad loans, as they did in the late 1990s by having extended loans to state-owned enterprises which were not able to repay, there will not be bank failures or bank runs because the Chinese commercial banks are owned by the government. Even today the government holds controlling shares of the major commercial banks. Therefore, Chinese citizens are not concerned about bank failures and the banks have no worries in extending loans. Furthermore, Chinese citizens save a high percentage of their income, about 40 percent. As a consequence the banks hold a large amount of deposits. That gives them sufficient liquid assets to extend loans to businesses. These are the reasons why China was not much affected during the 1997–1999 Asian financial crisis.

When the American economy slows down, demand for Chinese exports will decrease. This decreases aggregate demand in the Chinese economy and slows down the rate of China's economic growth. That is a major reason why in July the Politburo decided to change course on monetary policy, from restrictive to expansionary. At the same time the Chinese government has lost money from holding American assets (Treasury notes and stocks in financial institutions) which declined in value but this does not have much effect on the economy because the money was idle anyway. Since prices of American financial assets are so low, it may be prudent for the Chinese government to use its foreign reserve holding to purchase American assets. I cannot say that the prices of American assets are at their bottom, and nobody can, but it is reasonable to predict that in five years these assets will be more valuable than other foreign assets the Chinese government is holding. By buying a substantial amount of American financial assets, China will also help the US economy to recover.

37

What are the Shortcomings of the American Financial System?

The current global financial crisis originated in the United States. In the United States the financial crisis was the result of the bursting of the housing market bubble. The bubble occurred when the price of housing first went up substantially and then went down. The price of housing went up because many people decided to buy houses and it went down because people had to sell them. People bought houses because the consumers were willing to buy and the financial institutions were willing to finance their mortgages. The financial institutions were able to make money by financing the mortgages. The banks were not only using money from depositors to supply mortgages to the house buyers but were able to obtain financing by selling the mortgages to financial institutions which bought the mortgages and packaged them as stocks to sell to the public. Consumers were lured to buy the houses not only by the banks and financial institutions offering low but adjustable interest rates but also by the money they expected to earn when the prices of houses went up. The government played a role by encouraging the banks, especially Freddie Mac and Fannie Mae which they owned, to provide

easy money so that more Americans could own homes. The process started with banks and financial institutions willing to supply credit at low interest rates to consumers to buy houses. Once the process started the prices of houses went up more. Everyone involved could make more money. More houses were sold and the prices went even higher until there was no way to finance the purchase of more new houses.

Once the prices ceased to go up, all parties concerned were facing pressure to sell. Consumers living in houses which they could not afford except for the expectation of an increase in price found their mortgage interest rate going up. Some had to start selling their assets and put downward pressure on the prices of stocks. Other had to default on their monthly payments or even sell their houses. The banks could not make more money by selling mortgages directly to consumers or by refinancing through the stock market. Financial institutions holding stocks that consisted of mortgages as assets found that the incomes from these stocks were going down for the reason just stated. They had to sell the stocks and contributed to the downward movement of the stock market. The banks which owned mortgages directly lost money in the process. When every party – the consumers, the banks and the financial institutions – all lost money and were under pressure to sell their assets, the prices of stocks and of houses spiraled downward. Once the banks had too many bad assets in the form of default mortgages, they could not lend money to businesses for financing their payrolls and inventories. Production and employment decreased and the financial crisis led to a recession of the real economy. Unemployment increased.

Throughout the above story, there is an additional institution that exaggerated the bubble. This was the use of credit cards allowing the users to spend money that they did not have to buy things. When the price of housing moved up, the consumers became richer and spent more money to buy other consumer goods using credit cards. This exaggerated the upward movement of the bubble. When they became poor because of the increase in monthly mortgage payments, they curtailed their spending and thus led to less demand for consumer goods and an increase in unemployment. At the beginning of the financial crisis the consumers on average owed the issuers of credit cards about two and half months of their wage income.

My main purpose for retelling this familiar story is to point out the faults in the American financial system that enabled the housing bubble to occur. There are four elements. First, banks were allowed to use money other than their deposits to finance the mortgages that they issued. This enabled other financial institutions to issue stocks with housing mortgages as assets. Second, the banks were allowed to issue long-term mortgages at an adjustable interest rate. They could lure consumers into buying a house with financing at a low interest rate. Once the consumers purchased the house they could not get out of the contract when the banks increased the monthly interest payment. Third, there was no down payment required for a consumer to buy a house. Anyone with a steady job could buy a large house to live in and for speculation, without necessarily having any savings. This was a risky situation for the home buyer. Once the price of his house goes down, he goes bankrupt or the value of his assets becomes negative. Even if he manages to finance the monthly interest payment of his mortgages, he will have to curtail spending on other consumer goods. Fourth, consumers could use money that they did not have to buy consumer goods using credit cards. This is like 开空头支票 (writing a bad cheque). When they had to pay more for their mortgage they had to curtail other spending or default on their credit cards. Many consumers in the United States are now declaring bankruptcy because they owe the credit issuers money that they cannot repay.

The housing bubble and the financial crisis in the United States would not have occurred if the above four institutional arrangements had been forbidden. First, commercial banks should not sell mortgages to other financial institutions. Second, the interest rate on long-term mortgages should be fixed and not be adjusted. Third, consumers should not be allowed to purchase a house without paying at least 15 percent as down payment. Fourth, consumers should not be issued credit cards which allow them to spend money which they do not have.

Twenty-five years ago, all four rules were being practiced substantially, even if not required legally in the United States. Commercial banks used money mainly from depositors to lend to purchasers of houses or to business enterprises. The interest rate on mortgages was always fixed and could not be adjusted. There was always a down payment required for the purchase of a house. Users of credit cards had a limit on the amount they could spend monthly and had to pay their debt at the end of the month before using the card for spending again. All these rules have been broken in the last decade. If they had remained in force, the financial crisis would not have occurred.

In China, all four rules are enforced. Hence, China does not experience a serious financial crisis as does the United States.

38

What is the Nature of the American Financial Crisis?

A financial crisis occurs when the value of financial assets collapses. Financial assets include stocks and loans held by individuals and financial institutions. These assets entitle the owner to get something valuable in the future. For example, a stock issued by a corporation entitles its owner to receive future dividends or to sell it in the future for money. A mortgage loan entitles a bank to receive future income or interest from the borrower. When many financial assets in the entire economy become almost worthless, consumers will lose money and cannot buy consumer goods; banks and other financial institutions will not have enough money to lend to producers to pay their workers or to carry the inventories required to operate the business. Workers will be laid off, leading to fewer purchases of consumer goods. The chain reaction can cause a serious recession or even a depression.

To understand a financial crisis, we have to understand why prices of financial assets can go down by so much. The first answer is that prices of all assets, including physical assets like houses, can go down because of speculation.

When the prices of houses go up because of an increase in demand, speculators may believe that the prices will go up further and buy more houses. This in turn raises the prices even more, until people are not willing or able to buy more or some owners start selling them to make a profit. This is the beginning of the collapse in the prices of houses or the end of a speculative bubble of the housing market.

The most important point in this paper is that there is an additional reason, besides speculation, for the collapse of financial assets, which is absent for physical assets. The reason is that financial assets are promises to pay, to buy something or to sell something at a given price. This promise may not be backed by any physical assets. One early example is a promise to sell wheat at a given price in the future. The buyer of this promissory note needs wheat in the future and wants to be sure that he can buy it at a certain price. The seller of the note is taking a chance that the price of wheat will not be much higher so that he can make money by selling this promissory note. The promissory notes are called "wheat futures." Another example is a note promising the holder to be able to buy a stock of a corporation at a given price in a future date. The buyer of this note gets such a guarantee and the seller is taking a chance that the price of the stock will not go up by more than the difference between the current price (at which the he can acquire the stock to sell to the note holder in the future if necessary) and the price of that note. Such a note is called a "stock option." Both "futures" and "options" are examples of "derivatives" because their values are derived from the promises to buy or sell the underlying basic assets like wheat and corporate stocks. Note that financial derivatives can be further created at a higher level as promissory notes to buy or sell lower-level financial derivatives.

The possibility for the prices of financial derivatives to collapse is higher than for the prices of physical assets and of stocks because they fluctuate much more. Imagine that an IBM stock is priced at $100 now and an option to buy an IBM stock at $101 six months from now is worth $3. When the IBM stock goes up to $102, that option may go up to $4.5 or by a much larger percentage. If you invest in options, you may double or even triple your money but you may lose the entire investment. Furthermore, because the derivatives can be created out of little capital, their total value can be very large. In the US in the fall of 2008, the total value is more than four times the total value of all corporate securities, amounting to over $45 trillion, as compared with a national income of some $14 trillion, and twice the size of the entire US stock market. Since 2000, the total value of credit default swaps has ballooned from $900 billion to more than $45.5 trillion – roughly twice the size of the entire United States stock market. When the prices of these derivatives can go down by a large amount easily and when their total value is very large, the amount of money lost can therefore be very large, leading to a serious financial crisis. As an example, AIG issued promissory notes to financial institutions to guarantee the values of their financial assets including derivatives, and the company collapsed when the values of these assets went down. It takes tens of billions of dollars to bail out a financial institution like AIG. The basic cause of the problem is the ability of financial institutions like AIG to issue promissory notes without sufficient funds to back them up, just like an issuer of a stock option can create and sell the option without much financial backing. The ability to create and sell financial derivatives without much underlying capital to support them is the root cause of the current financial crisis.

To be fair to the financial institutions that trade financial derivatives, they try to protect themselves by hedging. Hedging means buying or selling two kinds of assets with prices going up and down in opposite directions. If I sell a future or an option for the buyer to be able to buy some commodity or stock at a given price in the future, I will also sell a future of an option whose price is expected to go in the opposite direction. When I lose money on one I will make up from the other. A problem with hedging is that I need to know the prices at which stocks go in opposite directions. My knowledge is based on historical

movement of these prices but the movement may change. A typical form of hedging is buying some assets and short-selling assets of similar types. When the prices of the first group go down I lose money on what I have purchased but make money by buying back the second group of assets at a lower price. (A more sophisticated form of hedging is for me to hold opposite positions on the same type of financial assets. When their prices go up together I may be long on some and short on others.) Even then, there will be unexpected price movements that will cause me to lose a lot of money. Otherwise, knowledge of hedging would be a guarantee of financial success and such a guarantee does not exist as long as price movements of financial assets are essentially unpredictable.

Is the trading of such financial assets a basic problem of a market economy? The first principle of a free market economy is that free trade or free exchange between two parties will make both parties better off; otherwise they will not trade voluntarily. Can we apply this principle to the trading of derivatives? The answer is no. Some economists favoring the free market system believe that gambling is a good thing because it is a free exchange between two parties. The present case is not just gambling; one party of the gamble does not have the money to pay when he loses. When a party sells a promissory note to another party, he may not have any funds to back up his future promise when necessary. This is the case of gambling without capital – I bet that it will not rain tomorrow but if it rains I will not have money to pay my bet. Selling some promises which one cannot afford to fulfill when required is harmful to society. The total quantity of such promises in an economy can be increased without limit unless their creation is regulated by the government. The prices of these promises can collapse easily and lead to a serious financial crisis. The lack of regulation in the creation of financial derivatives is the root cause of the current financial crisis in the US. The US government is now in the process of designing some suitable regulations for the financial markets including the trading of financial derivatives.

39

Why was Obama Elected President of the United States?

Barack Obama was elected President in the evening of November 4. The election was a landslide, with Obama receiving 365 electoral votes as compared with McCain's 173. In the democratic system of the US, the President and members of Congress are elected directly by the people. In China's democratic system, the top leaders of the Communist Party and the members of the National People's Congress are both elected indirectly, with direct election at the lowest level and members at higher levels elected by those immediately below. The result of this election is an important historical event because it is the first time that an African American has been elected, contrary to the expectations of almost all citizens half a year ago. The result has two implications. First, the vast majority of the American people are willing to select an African American as President, showing that racial prejudice has declined. Second, and more important, Obama is a political genius. No other black American could have been elected. He is young and has been in politics for only a short time. He was a little-known junior US Senator for only three years, and before that only a State Senator of the State of Illinois. At the beginning of the primary election of the Democratic Party to select its candidate for President, Senator Hillary Clinton was almost sure to win because she was much better known as a Senator and a former First Lady and she had a powerful political power base in the Democratic Party to support her. Coming out of nowhere, Obama won the election in one state after another. After a very close election Obama became the Democratic Candidate for Presidency in September.

After he became the Democratic Candidate, several factors contributed to his success in being elected President. The first is the economic crisis. Statistical studies have shown that the economic conditions are an important factor determining the result of a presidential election. Good economic conditions favor the incumbent or the candidate from his party; poor economic conditions favor the party not in power. Economic conditions are very bad during the current financial crisis, a subject I discussed in a previous article. The second is that Bush was the most unpopular president in many years, with below 30 percent of the voters considering his performance as President to be satisfactory. Besides the bad economic conditions, another major reason was his mishandling of the war in Iraq. Obama was favored partly because he had objected to the Iraq War from the beginning and declared that he would bring most troops home as soon as feasible if elected. One of his strategies to win was to associate his opponent Senator John McCain with Bush's failed policies. He also emphasized solving the pressing economic problems while McCain ran a negative campaign by telling voters that Obama was inexperienced, favored high taxes and was willing to surrender in Iraq.

The economic policies of Obama were criticized by distinguished conservative economists for two major reasons. First, he is in favor of a higher income tax rate for the rich and a lower rate for lower-income families. He favors having the government spend more to solve domestic problems. Second, on foreign trade he sees limits to free trade and is willing to impose restrictions on trade for specific countries. On health insurance policy, he favors increasing government provision to cover most and eventually all American citizens while McCain would favor more private insurance according to the choice of the individual. Both favor promoting energy independence by drilling along the coast and by supporting research on alternative energy sources to oil and coal. Both want to improve primary and secondary education in the US because the students' performance is low compared with many other, even less developed countries. In their debate on this topic, Obama received much approval when he said family education should be emphasized and asked voters not to let their children spend too much time watching TV or playing video games. Given the above proclaimed policies during an election, the reader should note that in the past, presidents often have not carried out the policies promised during the election campaign.

In the US, many people believe in the proposition of Thomas Jefferson that "the government is the best which governs the least." They think that, besides providing law and order, the government should not interfere with the activities of the people in pursuing their happiness freely. People in China tend to believe that the government should serve the people by providing leadership and welfare. Obama also believes that it is the duty of the President to provide leadership to the country in dealing with many problems, including reducing racial prejudices and working together to solve the country's financial crisis and other economic and social problems. He has the ability to provide such leadership which the US needs in living through the current financial crisis. He thinks of America as one country, often stating in his campaign speeches that we are not Republicans or Democrats, men or women, blacks or whites, Christians or Jews, but Americans when dealing with important issues facing the United States.

Some 70 percent of Europeans favor Obama over McCain as President. A possible reason is that his foreign policy is based on a more global view of the world. He was born in Hawaii in 1961 but spent four years around the age of 10 in Indonesia. This experience of living in a foreign country has provided him with viewpoints different from the purely American. Many Americans who have lived only in the United States can think only from the American point of view, which often means that the American way is the right way for all people in the world. The attitude of President Bush and his top cabinet members to spread the American form of democracy in the Middle East is a typical example of this American attitude. Obama's viewpoint is broader. He has more modesty and does not think that the American way is the best for every country, and he is unlikely to impose the American way on other countries. He is more willing to negotiate with foreign leaders who disagree with him.

Obama has other talents. When two of his former schoolmates at Harvard Law School were interviewed on TV, they said, "there were many very smart people at Harvard Law School but Obama stood out above all the rest." I can believe the truth of this statement since other evidence supports his genius. He was able to get so much enthusiastic support from so many people. The amount of contributions to his campaign broke the historical record. In the last few weeks of the presidential campaign he had so much contributed money that he was able to spend about four times the amount spent by McCain. I have heard him speak on TV many times and was much impressed by the substance of his speeches, including in particular one on the problem of racial prejudices in the United States. This was a very difficult subject for an African American to speak about. He showed an understanding of the non-blacks who had racial prejudices and of the blacks with bitter resentment, but he was able to make a convincing argument for them to work together to reduce racial prejudices for the benefit of both.

How will his talent help improve China–US relations? From the above we can conclude that his policy towards China will be based more on understanding, or at least an attempt to understand if he does not already understand China now, than on imposing the American way. He will not consider fighting terrorism as the only objective to achieve in America's relations with other countries. He is more open-minded than most previous Presidents and willing to accept good ideas from China for cooperation if they are presented to him. The Chinese government can take this opportunity to have an open dialog with his new administration on all economic, diplomatic and military issues. I hope and believe that relations between the two countries will improve and their cooperation will benefit both countries and humankind.

40

How will Obama Set his Policies for Economic Recovery?

This is an exciting time for the US and for the world now that Obama has been elected President. The world is facing a financial crisis and the US is experiencing a serious recession. The most important task for Obama is to deal with the economic recession and to deal with it quickly.

Before his inauguration in January, Obama cannot take action to improve the economy. Even announcing his economic policy would undermine the authority of President Bush. He cannot be silent about his future policy because the current problems are urgent. In the meantime President Bush and his administration are observing the development of Obama's policy decisions and do not want to act to undermine his future policy, or to limit his actions in the future. Consider the example of how to spend the 700 billion dollars to rescue the troubled financial institutions, corporations, the real estate sector and the home owners, a subject which I discussed in a recent article in this paper. Treasury Secretary Paulson cannot commit too much spending and fail to leave enough for the new administration. In addition, he is facing a delicate balance between public and personal interests. Acting to promote public interest itself is already difficult because of the need for immediate action and the need to leave room for the next administration to act. From the viewpoint of his personal interest, Secretary Paulson would not want to spend too much because he will be blamed if the economy shows no sign of recovery or perhaps even becomes worse after his action is taken. He would not want to spend too little because he will be blamed for not taking action when needed.

A safe strategy for Paulson and for the Bush administration is to consult with Obama's transition team and let the policies before inauguration be treated as the result of the deliberation of both administrations. This strategy is also good for Obama because it would allow him to act quickly without undermining Bush's authority. That is why the Bush administration and the Obama transition team are having joint meetings on important matters. Members of Obama's transition team are invited to attend important meetings of the Bush administration on national security, the economy and other matters of national interest. At these meetings Obama does not want to be identified too closely with the policies of the Bush administration, including the bailout package because in his opinion some policies are not well formulated and may fail.

What are the important economic policies that Obama has to deal with immediately? There are four major ones.

1. Policy on government expenditures to stimulate the economy. Soon after the US economy experienced a serious depression in the early 1930s, Keynes published *The General Theory of Employment, Interest and Money* in 1936 to suggest the use of government expenditure to increase aggregate demand in the macroeconomy. This has become the fiscal policy often used to regulate macroeconomic activities. The second component of macroeconomic policy consists of monetary policies which affect interest rate and money supply. We should await with interest the announcements of the Obama team or administration on what types of public infrastructure projects to finance. During the Eisenhower

administration, many federal highways were built to increase aggregate demand. Today old highways could be repaired or upgraded. American railroads could also be modernized. The speed of American trains is much lower than the best in the world.

The Chinese government has also increased government expenditures to simulate the economy. During the Asian financial crisis of 1998–99, Premier Zhu Rongji increased government expenditures on highways, railroads and projects connected with the Western Development Strategy. On November 9, the State Council announced ten major policies to stimulate economic growth. These include policies on infrastructure building, taxes and income subsidies that are also in Obama's plan to speed up economic recovery. Policies on health, education and environment are on both China's and Obama's agendas.

2. The government will spend money to rescue the financial markets and the real estate sector. As I pointed out in the previous essay on financial crisis, how to spend the 700 billion dollars is a difficult problem. Which private economic institutions should be rescued? How much should be paid for each rescue effort? How can the government avoid the "moral hazard" problem of encouraging future financial institutions and consumers to take more risk and expect the government to bail them out? Spending part of the rescue money is not classified as fiscal policy because the latter refers to spending money for the government's own economic activities. Neither is it monetary policy because monetary policy regulates the rate of interest and the supply of money for the economy as a whole and is not directed at individual financial institutions or consumers. There is some sentiment that more money should be spent to bail out consumers in danger of having their houses foreclosed than to bail out the rich financial institutions. The former requires that the income of each potential beneficiary be checked. Otherwise those who can afford their mortgage

payments will claim that they cannot in order to receive bailout benefits. The latter faces the difficult problems of selecting the appropriate beneficiaries and of making sure that they will use the money to extend loans to businesses and consumers.

A current monetary policy in the US is for the Federal Reserve to purchase commercial papers directly from private enterprises, rather than the traditional indirect way of trying to increase the ability of commercial banks to do so. However, in the US the Federal Reserve System is independent of the executive branch of the government headed by the President, unlike the Chinese case where the People's Bank is part of the State Council under the direction of the Prime Minister. Since I am discussing the policies of Obama, a policy of the Federal Reserve is not the subject of this article.

3. The government will also spend money directly to increase the income of poor consumers by extending their unemployment and food stamp benefits. All possibilities to improve the conditions of consumers will be considered carefully by Obama's team, including the policy he announced in his campaign to lower the taxes of low- and middle-income workers. The Obama government will provide aid to states and assistance for the troubled automotive industry.

4. Obama can help revive the economy simply by influencing the psychology of the Americans. Through his leadership he can increase the people's confidence that the economic future is good. President Franklin D. Roosevelt made a famous speech during the Great Depression, saying, "The only thing we have to fear is fear itself." If people have confidence in the economic future, there is no need to worry about the economic future. Government policies can change expectations and expectations will change economic behavior. A good leader can improve economic expectations which are important in determining the speed of economic

recovery. Obama is in a position to inspire the American people to work toward a more prosperous economy.

Finally, Obama has announced that the current American economy is in a serious recession and no policy can lead to a rapid recovery in a short time. I believe that Obama has assembled or will soon assemble some of the best people to help him set his policies and carry them out. We can hope that his leadership and the economic policies of his administration will be as good as possible under the present difficult circumstances.

41

Should the American Government Bailout the Automobile Industry?

The Big Three American auto companies, General Motors, Ford and Chrysler, are in financial trouble. They may go bankrupt. Should the government bail them out?

In principle, in the US market economy, the government only provides the rules of the game for private enterprises to operate and should not interfere with their operations if they follow the rules. If the economy is in a recession, the government may spend money to purchase goods produced by the private enterprises or even operate its own projects for the building of economic infrastructure, but should not get involved in the operations of the private enterprises themselves. One major exception is to rescue a large company if its failure will harm the entire economy severely. Chrysler was bailed out once when it was in trouble because the government feared that its failure would cause economic instability. Now the government has decided to bail out the financial industry because its failure will affect the functioning of the entire economy.

Whether the government should bail out the American automobile industry today depends on whether its failure will harm the economy significantly and whether a bailout will save it. The answer to the first part of the question is subject to the following deliberation. The failure of the Big Three American auto companies will always harm the economy in the short run by creating more unemployment but by how much will the economy be hurt? Should we let an enterprise fail and allow the human and physical resources of the country go elsewhere to be used more productively? By doing so, we allow competition to promote efficiency and progress in a market economy. Whether we should accept the pain in letting a few enterprises fail in exchange for the gain in making the economy more productive in the long run is always a difficult question to answer.

If the answer to the first part of the question is positive, we ask whether the enterprises can actually be saved. If the enterprises cannot be saved, there is no point in spending money to bail them out. In the case of the Big Three auto companies today, some have argued that there are basic structural problems which are so serious that it is impossible for the government to save them. The structural problems include the incompetence of the management, having evolved through years of monopolistic protection, and the high wages paid to workers under contracts with the United Automobile Workers union. By contrast, several Japanese automobile companies, including Toyota and Honda, producing cars in the US have better management and pay much lower wages in the absence of contracts with labor unions. If the structural problems are really serious and cannot be solved, there is no way that a bailout plan will work.

Proponents of a bailout plan have to convince the Bush government and members of Congress first that the failure of the automobile companies will seriously affect the American economy and, second, that a bailout plan will work. I say the Bush administration because Secretary Paulson already has

$700 billion bailout approved by Congress to spend and can use a part of it for the auto companies. I say the Congress because members of Congress can object to the way the approved money is used and, if the money was approved to bailout only financial institutions, Congress can approve more money for the automobile industry. The testimony in Congress on November 18 was about the two questions above, with Secretary Paulson objecting to a bailout for the auto industry and the CEOs of the three auto companies arguing in favor. Members of Congress expressed different opinions.

President-elect Obama has committed himself to helping the American automobile companies. The labor unions have supported candidates of the Democratic Party for presidency for years and supported the election of Obama in particular. During his campaign for the presidency, Obama said that he would promote the welfare of the middle class in the US including the workers. When he takes office as President he will almost surely try to bailout the automobile industry. The companies may go bankrupt before he takes office on January 20, however.

If the companies survive and Obama decides to bail them out, what would be a good plan? The currently suggested bailout plan is to extend loans to the auto companies at low interest rates. It may not work if the companies simply use the money to settle current debts and not to improve operations. To insure that the money will be used to increase production and employment, I suggest that the money be used as a subsidy to consumers intending to buy automobiles. When a consumer buys a car from the big three American companies, he would receive a subsidy of 20 percent of the purchase price, or he gets a 20 percent discount paid by the government. Thus the automobile companies can benefit only if they produce more cars. Obama would like to promote energy-efficient cars to solve America's energy and environmental problems. This plan can be combined with the automobile bailout plan by giving more subsidies to purchasers of energy-efficient cars. The plan should have a time limit, say for six months only, to be followed by a subsidy of 10 percent for another six months. Knowing that the time of the discount is limited, consumers will rush to buy and the auto companies will get relief immediately and substantially. The plan cannot last too long because a permanent subsidy will allow the auto companies to operate inefficiently for a long time. I have discussed this plan with an economic adviser to Obama. He told me that it is a good idea but it may be illegal to single out particular companies (excluding Toyota and Honda) to help with the subsidy. He suggested that we may get around this problem by giving subsidies only to those companies that made a loss in the last two years, for example.

It will be interesting to follow further developments of this story to learn how the American economy works and how politics affects the functioning of the American economy. In the decision process the Chinese government appears to be more efficient. On November 9, the State Council announced a plan to spend almost 600 billion US dollars to increase aggregate demand in order to prevent a large reduction in the growth of China's GDP while the US government is taking its time to debate what to do with the failing automobile industry.

42

The Excitement of Obama's Inauguration

Just a few days ago, my article in this column was critical of the West. It was about the biased opinion in the West about the Chinese economy. Today my article is positive about the United States of America. The country is full of excitement as never before, at least since I came to the United States 61 years ago. Several days before Obama's inauguration on January 20, the television news channels covered almost nothing except the anticipation and preparation of the inauguration, aside from slight interruptions from the miracle that a skillful pilot saved all passengers on board an airplane with two malfunctioned jet engines, that had caught flying geese, by landing the plane on the Hudson River and from the truce gestures of the Israeli and Palestinian governments. There was the train ride on January 18 of the President-elect and Vice President-elect and their spouses from Philadelphia to Washington DC, the same ride that President-elect Abraham Lincoln had taken before his inauguration. There were stops on the way to meet with and speak to large crowds of well-wishing people...

People are speculating what the main statements or most memorable quotes will be in obama's inaugural speech. For example, Franklin Roosevelt said, "The only thing we have to fear is fear itself." John F. Kennedy said, "Ask not what your country can do for you but what you can do for your country." In the case of Obama, the inauguration will be one of the great historical events even if he says nothing, just because he is the first African American to be elected President and he has already said enough during his campaign and after election to inspire the American people. However, being such a great orator, he will come up with an inspiring speech. Although rephrasing a few of the key statements in his past speeches would do very well, we can expect him to do better and make another extremely inspiring speech. About the possible comments, consider the central ideas of his message during the elections. Some of his favorite remarks during the campaign include: "This election is not about me but about you," "You made this success possible," and "Yes we can." Thus Obama's emphasis is on the Americans and not himself or on the "we" and not the "I." It is reasonable to expect that in his inaugural address he will emphasize the "we" or the "you" and not the "I" in accomplishing the daunting task of reviving the level of economic activities. In any case he will have something profound and inspiring to say. He knows that all eyes in the world are watching and what he says will be recorded in history books. He will not miss such a golden opportunity.

The hope and excitement of his inauguration has come at a time when America is suffering from the most serious economic downturn since the Great Depression in the early 1930s. However, the inauguration has brought out the Americans' hope more than their despair, their unity of purpose more than their division. Never before, except perhaps during World War II, have Americans been so united and so patriotic. In this country which is proud of its freedom and individualism, we see a sense of pride in belonging to a great nation and sharing the responsibility to promote the collective well-being. Such spirit may very well help the economy turn around sooner than otherwise. Americans now tend to think more about a larger world than their own. They may be able to provide world leadership not just by being powerful and self-centered but by feeling that all citizens in the world are one.

This is a very rare historical occasion where a truly great leader inspires, not for wishing to be a hero himself, but by the conviction that he is working for the good of his country with ideals that he believes in and for the people he loves. Obama is a leader who has the courage and ability to surround himself with the most talented people. In their special areas of expertise they are more knowledgeable and better informed than he is. He is a very good listener who can understand ideas of others and has an extremely able intellect to understand what others explain to him. He is a decisive leader who makes a decision after listening to different opinions. He is a very good organizer in bringing many people together to serve a common purpose, as witnessed by his organizational skills during the election campaign that led to victory after victory against unfavorable odds. He is cool and emotionally detached so as not to be seriously affected by disturbing circumstances. I have not seen a leader with all these qualities. He will turn out to be one of the greatest Presidents of the United States and one of the greatest leaders in the world.

As Obama himself pointed out, the economic and social problems of the United States are enormous and some will take even more than one four-year term of his presidency to overcome. However, the American people are now behind him in his effort to solve these problems. He will be given a "honeymoon period" of at least half a year to show the American people that his way will work. If it does not work, he will have difficulty in getting his agenda approved by Congress. It will be extremely exciting to watch the moves he will make after becoming President of the United States. This is truly the most exciting moment of American history that I have been fortunate enough to live through.

43

Are Obama's Economic Policies Essentially Correct?

It has been over half a year since Obama took office as President of the United States. Are his economic policies essentially correct?

Most economists in the United States think that the policies are correct. The reason is that during an economic downturn, when aggregate demand is lacking, the government should increase its expenditures to increase aggregate demand. Therefore the policies of the Obama administration to increase spending are correct. Economists in China would have a similar point of view. China is also experiencing a decrease in aggregate demand due to the reduction of exports. Economists agree that the Chinese government is right in increasing its expenditures.

I hope to discuss why some American economists think that the policies of the Obama administration are incorrect.

First, the particular expenditures proposed by the Obama administration may be incorrect if they interfere with the normal working of the market economy. For example, it is inappropriate to rescue the American automobile companies because this would affect competition in a market economy. A basic principle for the proper functioning of a market economy is to allow enterprises to make profits without subsidies given to specific enterprises from the government. A better policy would be for the government to subsidize the American consumers who will increase the purchase of automobiles of their choice. That way, the inefficient automobile manufacturers selling inferior products will not get the benefit of government subsidies.

Some may point out that the collapse of a large company would affect the entire economy. In the 1990s the American government tried to save Chrysler. Those who object to the rescue of American automobile companies today would also object to the rescue of Chrysler at that time. They would have let Chrysler suffer the consequences of its own mistakes.

Second, the timing of the increase in particular expenditures may be inappropriate. There are a number of economic projects that Obama declared that he would undertake while running for President. These include healthcare reform, the education of primary school students and the promotion of the development of clean energy. All require government spending. Those critical of his policies have said that this is not the time to be engaged in such projects when spending should be concentrated on those that would help increase employment or reduce unemployment the most.

Third, the total amount of expenditures is too large, leading to a level of government debt that is difficult to sustain. In 2009, the deficit of the federal government would amount to 12 percent of GDP. Even assuming future recovery, from 2011 to 2020, annual deficit is estimated to be about 4 to 5 percent of GDP. This is a larger percentage than in the period from 1970 to 2007, except for the year 1983. Such large deficits may lead to the lack of confidence of both domestic and foreign investors in American government bonds. Even if the government can pay the large debt in the future, it is not reasonable for the present generation to shift its burden to the future generation. A large increase in government debt will lower its value, the value of government debt, or increase the rate of interest which in turn will reduce investment for future economic development.

The Chinese government has exercised caution in increasing its debt. Historically its attitude has been to maintain a balanced budget as far as possible although in recent years it has allowed government debt to increase to some extent. In 2007 the total debt of the Chinese government amounted to only 18.4 percent of GDP when the American government debt was up to 60.8 percent, which further increased to over 70 percent in 2009. Those who support the large expenditures of the Obama administration believe that the large expenditures are appropriate during the current economic downturn.

So far, my topic is the fiscal policy of the American government and not the monetary policy of the Federal Reserve. The criticisms stated above are not directed at the monetary policy. For the purpose of increasing investment, the Federal Reserve has reduced the rate of interest substantially to almost zero. The Federal Reserve has also tried to rescue financial institutions, including the large banks, to enable them to extend loans to needy business borrowers who can then meet their payroll and carry their inventories and to needy consumers who can then maintain their consumption expenditures. It is claimed that allowing the banking system to fail would affect the proper functioning of the entire economy. This is different from allowing the automobile companies to fail as that would only affect the functioning of inefficient enterprises. Not all economists agree on this distinction.

Economists often disagree on the efficacy of particular economic policies. The reason is that there are many factors affecting the outcome of economic events in a complicated way. Furthermore, the value judgment of an economist may influence his opinion as well. One example is whether we should shift the burden of our debt to our children. Years later, when economists review the policies of the Obama administration with more data, their opinion may

still remain the same. If the economy recovers fairly rapidly the supporters will give credit to the policies and the critics will say that alternative policies would have led to an even faster recovery. If the economy recovers slowly the supporters will claim that alternative policies would have delayed the recovery even further. As George Bernard Shaw once remarked, the only thing we can learn from history is that we cannot learn anything from history. The speed at which the American economy shall recover is unlikely to influence the opinion of economists about the policies of the Obama administration.

44

The Serious Problems Facing Obama

I was a strong supporter of Obama during the presidential election and at the beginning of his presidency. In recent weeks his popularity has declined and many Americans do not support his major policies on healthcare, the war in Afghanistan and other issues such as the conflict between the Justice Department and the Central Intelligence Agency (CIA) on the treatment of detainees suspected to be terrorists during the Bush administration. According to public opinion polls, the percentage of American people who approved of Obama's performance as president decreased from 68 percent in April to 56 percent in early September. Many Americans today criticize him for trying to do too much at the same time, especially when the country is still experiencing a serious economic recession. I agree with their opinion. Allow me to explain.

First, healthcare reform was a major promise of Obama's during his campaign. In spite of the serious problems facing the American macroeconomy that needed to be solved, Obama decided to pursue healthcare reform immediately. The American system of healthcare provision and payment is complicated, having resulted from historical circumstances that cannot be explained in the space of this article. Through its power in accrediting medical schools, the American Medical Association was able to limit the number of trained doctors and thus increase the price of their services. When President Lyndon Johnson introduced Medicare as government-supported medical insurance for all senior citizens, the cost of healthcare increased immediately because demand for it increased while the supply was limited. The cost of healthcare is high also because hospitals want to collect as much payment as possible from the public and private insurance providers. Since the insurance providers want to minimize payment, they impose conditions for payment and increase the administrative cost for the hospitals. The American system of justice encourages people to sue unnecessarily because the plaintiff does not have to pay legal fees out-of-pocket and their lawyers are willing to collect a percentage of the payment only if they help win the case. This increases the cost of insurance for doctors to protect against being sued by patients for malpractice. The doctors pass a part of this cost to the patients or their insurers. They also have an incentive to overprescribe expensive medical tests to protect themselves against being sued for malpractice.

With all these problems in the background, a major objective of healthcare reform is to provide health insurance to all Americans, but who should provide the insurance and how to pay for it? People disagree, especially on whether the government should offer a public option for health insurance. Those in favor say that this would provide competition to private insurance and thus reduce cost. Those objecting claim that the competition is unfair and that insurance provided by the government, including Medicare for the elderly, has been too costly because of bureaucratic inefficiency. The controversy over how to reform healthcare, as expressed in heated debates in town-hall meetings, has seriously damaged Obama's presidency. On September 9, Obama addressed members of the entire US Congress on healthcare reform and made an excellent speech but the speech did not yield much more support from the

Republican members of Congress who objected to offering of a public option for health insurance. A healthcare reform bill will likely be passed in 2009 but the bill may be too weak and not worth the controversy and the use of Obama's political capital. His political capital could be used elsewhere to solve other urgent problems on the Obama agenda, including the serious recession, energy/environment and the low quality of education.

Second, many Americans do not agree with Obama's policy to expand the war in Afghanistan. I have devoted a recent article to explain the failure of this policy. Readers can understand why this policy is mistaken and why many Americans do not support it. Most recently the Afghanistan policy is being carefully reexamined but it is hard to find a solution that will satisfy most Americans.

Third, given that the respect for the law is essential in American society, many citizens object to the way possible terrorist detainees were treated during the Bush administration. Obama once said that he believed in justice but preferred to look forward to solve current problems rather than deal with past mistakes. However, the Justice Department is investigating into possible wrongdoings of previous CIA agents in the treatment of detainees. Some said that the use of harsh treatment was necessary and effective in forcing the terrorist detainees to tell the truth in order to help protect the lives and security of Americans. Others said that such harsh means were not effective, and even if they were, such actions violated American laws. No matter which side wins the debate, the Obama administration is weakened by the controversy.

Fourth, although in foreign policy Obama was very popular in Europe, he faces the same difficult problems as any other American President would in dealing with the conflict between Israel and its Arab neighbors, nuclear proliferation in countries like North Korea and Iran and the political conflicts in several African nations. Just extending a friendly hand and expressing willingness to negotiate may increase goodwill in some cases but are not sufficient to solve the difficult problems mentioned above.

The major slogan of the Obama presidential election campaign was "change." Change was welcomed by many citizens who were dissatisfied with the Bush administration. However, introducing too many changes at once may not be the right policy. There is a limit to the amount of change that a society, or any human organization, can absorb in a short time. Americans were ready to have a new and capable President but not ready to make changes in so many important issues like healthcare, promotion of clean energy, and an expansion of an unpopular war, especially when they are experiencing an economic crisis.

Whether Obama will receive popular support in the near future depends crucially on the extent of recovery of the American economy. From past experience and empirical studies, if the economic conditions are favorable, the party in power will be re-elected; otherwise the opposing party will win. If the American economy recovers quickly, Obama will get stronger popular support and some of these difficult problems will be more easily resolved.

About the Author

Gregory C Chow is Professor of Economics and Class of 1913 Professor of Political Economy, Emeritus, at Princeton University. He received a BA from Cornell, 1951, and a PhD from the University of Chicago, 1955, and served on the faculty of MIT, Cornell, Harvard and Columbia before joining Princeton in 1970 as the Director of the Econometric Research Program, which was renamed the Gregory C Chow Econometric Research Program in 2001. Prof Chow is a member of the American Philosophical Society and of Academia Sinica and a Fellow of the American Statistical Association and of the Econometric Society. He is the author of 14 books and over 200 articles, specializing in econometrics, dynamic economics, and the Chinese economy. Prof Chow has served as adviser to the government of Taiwan, the Prime Minister and the Commission for Reconstructing the Economic System of the PRC. He cooperated with the State Education Commission of the PRC to modernize economics education in China, where he holds honorary professorship at ten universities and was awarded three honorary doctor's degrees.

About the Author